Thomas Cranmer
Theologian

Thomas Cranmer Theologian

G.W. Bromiley

James Clarke & Co.

James Clarke & Co.

P.O. Box 60
Cambridge
CB1 2NT
United Kingdom

www.jamesclarke.co
publishing@jamesclarke.co

Hardback ISBN: 978 0 227 17873 7
Paperback ISBN: 978 0 227 17871 3
PDF ISBN: 978 0 227 17874 4
ePub ISBN: 978 0 227 17872 0

British Library Cataloguing in Publication Data
A record is available from the British Library

First published by The Lutterworth Press, 1956
This edition published by James Clarke & Co. 2023

Copyright © 1956 G.W. Bromley

All rights reserved. No part of this edition may be reproduced, stored electronically or in any retrieval system, or transmitted in any form or by any means, electronic, mechanical, photocopying, recording, or otherwise, without prior written permission from the Publisher (permissions@jamesclarke.co).

Contents

Introduction: The Reformer		vii
1	The Scholar	1
2	Scripture and Tradition	12
3	Justification	28
4	The Church and Ministry	42
5	Holy Baptism	57
6	The Eucharistic Presence	69
7	The Eucharistic Work	84
Concluding Estimate		97
Select Bibliography		104
Index of Subjects		105
Index of Names		106

Introduction: The Reformer

By Shakespeare's classification Thomas Cranmer was one of those who have greatness thrust upon them. Neither by birth, training, connections, nor opportunity could he expect to play any great part in the affairs of church or nation. Born in 1489 at Aslockton in Nottinghamshire, the second son of a small squire he had little option but to seek a career in the ministry. His early education under a "marvellous severe and cruel schoolmaster"[1] was not helpful, for as a result "he lost much of that benefit of memory and audacity in his youth that by nature was given to him, which he could never recover".[2] But his natural ability could not be destroyed, and when he proceeded to Cambridge he graduated B.A. with sufficient distinction to be awarded a fellowship in Jesus College and to follow the more serious reading in divinity which this entailed.

From his election to a fellowship to his sudden translation from the university the story of Cranmer was the quiet one of progress in academic learning, status and reputation. An early marriage – he was not yet in orders – threatened to interrupt his career,[3] for the statutes of the college did not allow married fellows. For a time Cranmer had to be content with a readership in Buckingham College (now Magdalene). But when his wife died in childbirth he was re-elected to his forfeited fellowship, and there were no further checks to his progress. He took his doctorate in divinity and for some years acted as examiner in the theological schools. He received and declined an invitation from Wolsey to serve in the newly founded Cardinal's College at Oxford. Already in the twenties he had that developed reputation as a scholar which would assure him of a minor eminence in his own sphere.

---

1. *Narratives of the Reformation*, pp. 238-239.
2. *Ibid., loc. cit.*   3. *Ibid.*, p. 269.

The years at Cambridge hardly prepared Cranmer for the onerous duties to which he was to be called, but they determined the use to which he would put his new opportunities. As the contemporary narrative has it, he had been "nozzled in the grossest kind of sophistry",[4] and he himself recalls "an ignorant reader, whose scholar I was in Cambridge some forty years passed, who, when he came to any hard chapter which he well understood not, he would find some pretty toy to shift it off, and to skip over unto another chapter, which he could better skill of".[5] But he quickly came under the influence of the new learning, and perhaps from Colet, or more likely from Erasmus, he acquired a new respect for the Bible,[6] and a taste for plain and simple exposition. His pursuits kept him well-informed in theological matters, and while he did not plunge hastily into Lutheran teaching, he could not ignore the doctrines for which Luther contended. Like all educated churchmen, he was also alive to the ecclesiastical abuses which Colet castigated so freely, and he seems to have come early to the conviction that no real progress would be possible until the power of Rome was broken.[7] Fundamentally, Cranmer had not moved very far from what we might call an enlightened orthodoxy, but he came to a wider sphere of ecclesiastical service with very definite views of the Bible and the Papacy, a general if not very decided sympathy with some of Luther's teaching, and the concern for an instructed faith.

By temperament, Cranmer would have been quite content to live out his days in the modest light of academic success. He had no desire for power or wealth. In reply to a later criticism of Cecil, he said quite honestly: "I am not so doted to set my mind upon things here, which neither I can carry away with me, nor tarry long with them."[8] Financially, indeed, a bishopric was no great attraction, for as he said in the same letter: "I took not half so much care for my living when I was a scholar of Cambridge, as I do at this present. For although I have now much more revenue, yet I have much more to do

---

4. *Ibid.*, p. 219.
5. P.S., I, p. 305.
6. *Narratives of the Reformation*, p. 219.
7. P.S., II, p. 327.
8. *Ibid.*, p. 437.

withal. ... And if I knew any bishop that were covetous, I would surely admonish him; but I know none, but all beggars."[9] Again, Cranmer had no great taste or aptitude for the ecclesiastical and political administration in which he was later to be enmeshed. He must have foreseen that his entry into the King's service would involve preferment, but if he looked for a reward it was that of "some smaller living, that he might more quietly follow his book".[10] When he learned that the King had actually marked him out for the archbishopric, he felt "a great inability to such a promotion, and was very sorry to leave his study".[11] At his examination he put it in this way: "There was never a man came more unwillingly to a bishoprick than I did to that,"[12] and there can be little or no doubt that he was telling the simple truth.

But although Cranmer was in every way fitted and prepared for a scholar's life, fate or circumstances or Henry VIII or the devil or providence – however we like to view it – had apparently decided otherwise. It all came about from a chance encounter in the summer of 1529. The plague had visited Cambridge as it so often did, and Cranmer retired with two of his pupils to their house at Waltham in Essex. While they were there, the King made a twofold visit to the house. It was just after the last and most vexatious delay in the so-called divorce, when on July 23 Henry had expected Campeggio to find in favour of a dispensation to annul the marriage, but a fresh turn in the complicated European situation had caused him instead to adjourn for the vacation. Cranmer did not see the King in person. There was no reason why he should. But he had a meal with his two Cambridge friends, Gardiner and Fox, who were both employed in the business. To these two he dropped his quiet but in its own way revolutionary suggestion, that since the legality or otherwise of the marriage with Katherine of Aragon was an academic question it should be decided by a majority opinion of the appropriate faculties of the Christian universities. Judgment could then be given accordingly in the English ecclesiastical courts without waiting

---

9. P.S., II, p. 437.
10. Ibid., p. 223.
11. Ibid., loc. cit.
12. Ibid., p. 216.

for Rome. Gardiner and Foxe had some doubts as to how Henry would receive the suggestion, so they took good care to throw the responsibility for it on Cranmer. But in his mood of exasperated frustration the King welcomed it with enthusiasm,[13] and it was only a matter of months before Cranmer was summoned to the court.[14] He did not at once abandon his academic career, but his days of scholarly seclusion were undoubtedly at an end.

In the King's service, Cranmer's first employment was entirely in relation to the divorce. His initial task was congenial enough. He simply had to state his own views of the question in writing as a basis for discussion and persuasion in the English universities. Cranmer's approach was purely academic and not in any sense personal. He believed that the marriage had in fact been invalid from the start. Henry had been permitted to marry his deceased brother's wife, but the Papacy had no authority at all to dispense against a clear ruling of Scripture. He not only stated this view but also defended it against the wit and eloquence of Reginald Pole, of whose book he had to admit that "in many things he satisfieth me very well".[15] He was also committed with the task of arguing out the case in Cambridge, and in 1530 he was attached to an embassy to Rome with the particular duty of broaching the matter in foreign universities and discussing it with the Pope. Finally, in 1531 he became ambassador to the Imperial Court with the special task of making contact with the German Lutherans and if possible enlisting their support. The results of all this activity were very mixed. As concerns his mission he made no headway with either the Pope or the Emperor, but he had some success not only in Cambridge but also in several foreign universities, helped no doubt by royal pressure in the one case and appropriate rewards in the others. For himself, he, received the archdeaconry of Taunton from Henry, the high-sounding office of Penitentiary for England from the Papacy, and a second wife, the niece of the reformer Osiander, from Lutheran Germany.

---

13. Foxe, VIII, p. 8.
14. *Narratives of the Reformation*, p. 242.

15. P.S., II, pp. 229 f.

It was while Cranmer was still in Germany that Archbishop Warham died, and with unusual celerity Henry nominated his ambassador to the vacant office. Normally, of course, the revenues of vacant sees formed a useful addition for a while to the royal treasury. But in this case there was an obvious reason for haste. Henry had already carried through legislation which had brought his relation with the Papacy to snapping point. Before the break came, he wanted a properly recognized archbishop who could give definitive sentence in his matrimonial suit. The choice fell on Cranmer, partly because he had suggested the course of action which Henry was now following, partly because he was so transparently sincere in his advocacy of the cause, and partly because he was not the character to try to impose his own policies or ideas on his royal master. It was not a popular choice either with the contemporaries of Cranmer whom he had suddenly outstripped, or, as we have seen, with Cranmer himself. Gardiner in particular seems to have found it extremely unwelcome, no doubt because he would have fancied the archbishopric himself. His resistance to the later visitation of Cranmer makes it quite plain that he did not take at all kindly to the overlordship of his one-time inferior.[16] But Cranmer himself did not want the office. He did everything in his power to avoid it, first prolonging his journey abroad, then trying to influence the King indirectly, and finally declaring quite plainly that he had scruples against the oath of loyalty to the Papacy.[17] But Henry had made up his mind, and all the obstacles raised were quickly overcome. To deal with the conscientious objections Henry devised a legal proclamation of reservation, of which the most that can be said perhaps is that it is better than the more common concealed and mental reservation.[18] Gardiner and others simply had to make the best of a situation which they could not alter. A judicious deployment of money ensured that the bulls came through with record expedition, and on March 30, 1533, Cranmer was installed in his new office.

His first duty as archbishop was to conclude the matrimonial suit which had first brought him into the royal service. This

---

16. Cf. P.S., II, pp. 304-305. 17. P.S., II, pp. 216-224. 18. P.S., II, p. 224.

did not take long. In accordance with the majority judgments of the universities the marriage was declared void in the archiepiscopal court. This was on April 23. Five days later the marriage between the King and Ann Boleyn was officially recognized and on September 10 Cranmer acted as sponsor for the baby Elizabeth. But the matrimonial difficulties of the King were not yet at an end and on three occasions the archbishop had to intervene again on Henry's behalf; first, to dissolve the marriage with Ann, then to break the unwelcome union with Anne of Cleves, and finally to report the infidelities of Katherine Howard.[19] For his activities in this sphere he had ample justification in law and precedent, but Cranmer himself obviously felt the distastefulness of his work, especially in relation to Ann Boleyn.[20] Not even his warmest advocate can enthuse over this side of his activity. Perhaps the chief point in his favour is that he was always pressing for a reform of the canon law which made this type of adventure possible. But not unnaturally he could never overcome the innate hostility of the civil rulers, who had no great desire for a stricter ecclesiastical discipline.

In the wider sphere of ecclesiastical affairs, Cranmer succeeded to a situation which had changed vastly since his first encounter with Henry. Acting conjointly, the King and Parliament had not only broken the various links with Rome, but brought the church at home under closer political control. Willingly or unwillingly, Warham himself, supported by Convocation, had "given the supremacy to Henry VIII, and said that he ought to have it before the bishop of Rome, and that God's word would bear him".[21] Temporarily the rejection of papal supremacy enhanced greatly the authority of Canterbury, but it was not long before Henry appointed an ecclesiastical vicegerent, and as concerns the larger administration of the church Cranmer had for the most part only an indirect and not a direct voice. Such measures as the suspension of annates and the ratification of Henry's lordship were carried through quite irrespective of the archbishop, although in matters of this kind Cranmer himself had no objections.

---

19. P.S., II, pp. 408-409.   20. P.S., II, pp. 323-324.   21. P.S., II, p. 215.

Indeed, he did a good deal to state the case for the royal as opposed to the papal supremacy. As distinct from Warham he had the advantage of sincerely believing it to be scriptural and therefore right. The dissolution of the monasteries was also outside the sphere of Cranmer's initiation or control. He had no great love for the monasteries, which had outlived their day and were centres of papal opposition.

But he could not approve, although neither he nor anyone else could arrest, the shameless spoliation of church property, which he himself would have applied exclusively to the endowment of new bishoprics, and works of scholarship and charity.[22] These matters, however, came under the more capable if more ruthless hands of Thomas Cromwell.

All the same, Cranmer was not by any means a spectator during these early years under Henry. His main work was done in much less striking ways, but in the long run it was no less influential. Not only did he argue against the papal supremacy, but he improved the occasion by attacking such specifically papal practices and doctrines as private masses and purgatory. He also initiated discussions with a view to a new doctrinal statement, and in the Ten Articles of 1536 and the more extended exposition usually known as the *Bishops' Book* there is a distinct if limited tendency in the direction of Lutheranism. At this time external events and the foreign policy of Cromwell favoured a Lutheran approximation, and Cranmer exploited the situation to the best of his ability. The injunctions of 1536 insisted on instruction in the Creed, the Lord's Prayer and the Ten Commandments, and in the years immediately following many famous shrines were dismantled, the number of saints' days was drastically reduced, and Lutheran "orators" were brought over with a view to political and theological alliance.[23]

But Cranmer's greatest achievement in this period was his successful introduction into the churches of an English Bible. Already in 1534 he had initiated the project of an officially revised version, but those bishops who were hostile to the project delayed it by obstruction. As a stop-gap, a licence was

---

22. P.S., II, p. 16.   23. P.S., II, p. 379.

procured for Coverdale's translation, but this was recognized to be only second-hand and inferior. Eventually, in August 1537, Cranmer came across a copy of the so-called Matthew's Bible, which consisted of all the work done by Tyndale completed by Coverdale. Whether or not Cranmer recognized Tyndale's hand it is difficult to say, but he certainly liked the version and sent it to Cromwell with a request to submit it to the King and if possible have it licensed for public reading.[24] When this was successfully done he wrote to Cromwell: "You have showed me more pleasure herein, than if you had given me a thousand pounds"; and he described Cromwell's part in the success as an action which would be remembered at the last day.[25] Rather typically, Cromwell took a financial interest in the publication. He had an eye for the earthly as well as the eternal treasure. It was soon realized, of course, that certain corrections would be necessary in the new version, but in its amended form Cromwell ordered that it should be set up in all parish churches. There was some delay in the carrying out of this order, for the printing was done in Paris and probably at the instigation of English bishops the work was interrupted by the Paris Inquisition. However, the Bible came out at last, and several editions were printed and circulated. Cranmer himself contributed a preface,[26] and for that reason it is often known as Cranmer's Bible. The title is a just one, for although many others had contributed to this notable reform, the interest of Cranmer was decisive. Of all his achievements in the earlier period, the introduction of the English Bible was perhaps the most far-reaching and influential.

So far conditions had been favourable to the archbishop, and if he looked back in 1539 he must have been astonished at the ground which had been traversed during the ten years since he had left Cambridge. Ecclesiastical control had passed out of the hands of the Papacy. Abuses due to the papal supremacy had been remedied. Ancient foundations and shrines were in process of dissolution.[27] The pattern of religious life and activity was changing. A beginning had been made not only with

---

24. P.S., II, p. 344.
25. P.S., II, p. 346.
26. P.S., II, pp. 118 f.
27. Cf. P.S., II, p. 378.

doctrinal revision but also with the dogmatic and ethical instruction of the people. The English Bible had been introduced into the churches and to some extent the homes and hearts of the nation. Cranmer himself could not claim credit or responsibility for all these changes. But it can hardly be denied that he had made skilful use of the situation to add the less tangible but no less important theological and religious renovation to the process of administrative and financial reform.

Nor was he without hope of even better things to come. Negotiations with the Lutherans were well under way. A matrimonial alliance with the reforming duchy of Cleves had been arranged. There was the possibility of further reform in both the doctrinal and ceremonial spheres, and Cranmer may even have hoped that he would soon be able to add to the English Bible an English Prayer Book.

As it turned out, however, Cranmer's main task during the rest of Henry's reign was to be one of defence rather than attack. For just at this juncture a variety of circumstances combined to bring about a complete reversal in religious policy. Perhaps the ultimate reason was the political, that the friendship of the Emperor had become more important than that of the Lutherans. But Henry's innate conservatism and his dislike for the dogma and dogmatism of the German orators made a change of this nature welcome to him. Again, he no doubt sensed the hostility of many of the people to too drastic reforms, and he could hardly ignore the very powerful resistance to Cromwell amongst the older nobility, both inside and outside the council. The final spur came with the arrival of Anne of Cleves, who unfortunately did not fulfil the high hopes held out by a flattering portrait. The more potent charms of Katherine Howard were only enhanced by comparison.

The first change came on the theological front with the adoption of six articles: transubstantiation, the vow of chastity, the private mass, auricular confession, the celibacy of the clergy, and the denial of the cup to the laity. Both in Parliament and Convocation Cranmer resisted this act to the very last,[28] but he was overborne by the King and the lay peers,

---

28. Foxe, VIII, pp. 14, 23; P.S., II, p. 168.

and he had no option but to submit. At first the act was not applied with any rigour and Cranmer himself had little to fear from it so long as he kept his more heterodox opinions to himself and concealed his wife. The attainder and execution of Cromwell had more serious consequences, for it deprived Cranmer of his main supporter, reversed the policy with which he had been identified, brought his most active opponents to power, and threatened ruin and disgrace to Cranmer himself.

Indeed, the odds in London were ten to one that Cranmer would share the fate of his lay colleague.[29] At the very least it was expected that a hostile vicegerent would be appointed, thus depriving him of all genuine power or influence. The hopes of Cranmer's enemies were all falsified by events, but with the fall of Cromwell the archbishop entered on a bitter and at first not very hopeful defensive.

Had he been more politically minded, Cranmer might easily have consumed these years in attempts at sheer self-preservation. On at least three occasions he was exposed to damaging attacks which had as their final end his downfall. The first time he was accused by his own prebendaries. The second, he was attacked in Parliament by a certain Gostwicke. The third, he was actually summoned by his fellow-members of the Council who intended to commit him to the Tower. Cranmer was not much more than a child when it came to this kind of warfare. He had the guileless nature which does not easily make plots or counter or unravel them. He had an implicit faith in the truth which in that turbulent age only the long-range perspective of history can justify, not the short-term perspective of immediate advantage. If he survived the attacks, it was not due to precautions taken or his power of counter-attack, but to the powerful protection of the King, who valued his loyalty and scholarship and seemed to have a strange affection for the man who was in almost all things his opposite.[30] At any rate, Henry quickly saw through the conspiracy of the prebendaries and turned it against its authors.[31] When he

---

29. Deane, *Thomas Cranmer*, p. 148.
30. Cf. *Narratives of the Reformation*, pp. 258-259; Pollard, *Thomas Cranmer*, p. 159.
31. *Narratives of the Reformation*, p. 252.

Introduction: The Reformer

heard of Gostwicke's attack he threatened that if he did not apologize to the archbishop he would soon make him a poor gosling – he had profited greatly by the dissolution.[32] He even gave Cranmer a ring which brought confusion to the Council, and rated his advisers for their unjustifiable and discourteous treatment of his most trusted servant.[33] Without this patronage, the outlook for the archbishop would have been black indeed.

As it was, his survival was important, for now that there was no vicegerent the archbishop had a greater influence in religious matters, and he could use his power to ward off the various counter-attacks and even to make one or two advances. He was not uniformly successful. The revision of the *Bishops' Book* took a reactionary direction which Cranmer could not resist, in spite of one or two minor victories. And this time the book came out not merely with the approval of Convocation but with the sanction of Parliament and the Crown. Again, he could not prevent a progressive restriction of the English Bible. New editions of the Great Bible ceased after 1541, and in 1543 the Tyndale version was proscribed and various classes were forbidden to read the Bible at all.[34] On the other hand, Cranmer thwarted a very serious attempt to revise the Great Bible, which would probably have resulted in its complete withdrawal. The matter was taken out of the hands of a committee appointed by Convocation and remitted to the universities, who seem quietly to have done nothing. It was not unimportant that the Great Bible did at least remain even if it was no longer widely circulated or read.

Again, Cranmer enjoyed one or two lesser triumphs, especially in the liturgical sphere. He successfully resisted a legalization of all existing uses. In this way the principle of uniformity was safeguarded and many customs and ceremonies remained unauthorized. He even made an attempt to "purge the antiphoners and mass-books of all apocryphas, feigned legends, superstitions, ovations, collects, versicles and responses", together with references to the bishop of Rome and non-authenticated saints.[35] In the same field, Cranmer even had the

---

32. Foxe, VIII, p. 27.
33. *Narratives of the Reformation*, pp. 254 f.
34. Foxe, V, p. 527.
35. Wilkins, *Concilia*, III, p. 863.

opportunity to introduce a little English. Special litanies were ordered in view of the bad harvest of 1543 and the French War of 1544,[36] but they were not very well attended, and to stimulate interest Henry ordered an English translation.[37] At first, the Latin was translated directly, but Cranmer himself attempted a very free rendering[38] which was published the following year and by royal proclamation replaced all existing litanies. In this way the first part of the English Prayer Book came out even during the period of reaction, and already Cranmer displayed to the full those qualities of liturgical craftsmanship which he would reveal on an even greater scale in the completed work. The Litany is not used to-day as it still deserves to be used, but no one can easily deny either the comprehensiveness of its petitions, the balance of its structure, or the terseness and yet also the majesty and cadence of its phrasing.

The French War had rather curious effects on the ecclesiastical situation. On the one hand, Henry needed money, so he began to plunder the chantries. On the other hand, he needed the friendship of the Emperor, so he maintained the various ceremonies which Cranmer was trying to abolish.[39] In the autumn of 1546, the situation took a sudden turn in the archbishop's favour, for the religious war in Germany brought England and France together and there was talk of a thoroughgoing reformation in both countries in opposition to the Papacy and the Empire. Whether this project would have been realized it is difficult to say. Hooper thought it at least a possibility,[40] and Cranmer was certain of it. The matter was obviously discussed, and there is no doubt that the traditionalists, and especially Gardiner and the Howards, were all under a cloud. But the new development was not destined to come under Henry, for in January 1547 his turbulent life came to an end. In his last hours it was to his trusted friend the archbishop that he turned for spiritual comfort.

The death of Henry opened up a new era for Cranmer and his work, although he himself did not view it in that light.[41]

---

36. P.S., II, p. 493.
37. P.S., II, p. 494.
38. P.S., II, p. 412.
39. P.S., II, p. 415.
40. *Original Letters*, I, p. 41.
41. P.S., II, p. 415, n. 5.

By his will, Henry had appointed a council of regency, on which the reforming party had a clear majority. The weakness as Cranmer saw it was the lack of a strong and securely acknowledged leader, and the consequent danger of faction. But he could hardly have found a more sympathetic ruler than the Protector Somerset, who for all his faults and the weakness of his economic policy had generous ideas and sincere reforming convictions. Under Somerset Cranmer had a fairly free hand in more specifically religious and theological matters, and he used the opportunity to go forward with slow but penetrating changes. By temperament Cranmer was cautious and conservative. He came slowly to his own convictions, and he did not attempt to press them hastily on others. He was content to wait both for favourable circumstances on the one hand and a leaven of instruction on the other. His aim was not to sectionalize the church and nation, but if possible to carry them with him, reforming not merely by edict from without but by renewal from within. In this policy he had the enthusiastic support of the Protector.

A first task was to restrain the more revolutionary elements, who took advantage of Henry's death to initiate violent propaganda and even to invade churches and manhandle priests. All the same, in his own way Cranmer encouraged a progressive policy. A special course was selected for the Paul's Cross sermons. The *Paraphrase* of Erasmus was published in English, and the first book of *Homilies* was circulated. The injunctions of 1547 encouraged this tendency. It was insisted that once at least in each quarter there should be a sermon and that the rudiments of the faith should be definitely taught in English. The Bible and the *Paraphrase* had to be made available, and at the mass the Epistle and Gospel were to be read in the vernacular.[42] In Convocation the cup was at last conceded to the laity,[43] and Parliament opened up a period of freer discussion with its repeal of the six articles and the heresy laws. A new chantries bill was opposed by Cranmer, who disapproved although he could not prevent the misappropriation of church endowments by the rapacious nobility.

---

42. P.S., II, pp. 498 f.   43. P.S., II, p. 511.

The granting of the cup to the laity made an opening for the reconsideration of the whole communion office, and Cranmer would have liked a fairly large-scale revision in accordance with his changing doctrine. For the moment, however, he was foiled by the other bishops and could only add to the existing mass a definite communion and some concluding prayers in English. In 1548 various ceremonies were ended by proclamation, and in the spring Westminster and St. Paul's took the lead by substituting an English communion for the Latin mass. To further the instructional side of the work Cranmer issued a translation of the Latin catechism of Justus Jonas. This Lutheran work was a disappointment to some of the more advanced reformers, who did not notice, perhaps, that Cranmer had made some careful alterations to avoid a doctrine of consubstantiation. The eucharistic controversy was becoming so violent and unseemly at this time that temporarily even licensed preachers were allowed only to read the official homilies.[44] But Cranmer himself was now coming to a definite mind on this issue on which he had hesitated for so many years. The main impetus to a Reformed view seems to have come from Ridley, who convinced him that the medieval interpretation of the real presence was an illegitimate development of the biblical and patristic teaching.[45] But he was finally helped by the continental scholars who had now accepted his offer not only of refuge but of useful employment in England. Peter Martyr especially had many conversations with him on this issue,[46] and in Martyr he found a scholar whose training, outlook and interests were wholly congenial.

The wider contacts of Cranmer are almost a subject in themselves, and he emerges as one of the genuinely ecumenical figures of the century. From his early visit to Nuremberg he had maintained sympathetic contact with the German Lutherans, and he made it his business to keep in touch with all the writings of contemporary scholars. When the victories of Charles V and the imposition of the Interim made conditions extremely difficult for many continental reformers he invited them to England and found for them strategic posts where

---

44. P.S., II, p. 513. 45. P.S., II, p. 218. 46. P.S., I, p. 374.

Introduction: The Reformer

they could influence the present and future course of events. Fagius, Bucer, Martyr, Tremellius, Ochino, John a Lasco and others were indebted to this hospitality. But beyond that Cranmer had the idea of a full-scale protestant synod where the various reforming churches could come to a common mind and issue a common confession of faith. With a view to convening some such synod he wrote letters to Melanchthon, Bullinger and Calvin,[47] but Melanchthon seemed very reluctant to do anything and practical difficulties prevented the realization of the project. The failure was not due to any lack of enthusiasm or effort on the part of Cranmer. If his plan had been adopted, it might have had very beneficial consequences for the evangelical cause both in England and elsewhere.

With the introduction of an English communion service, the demand for liturgical revision became more insistent, and the way opened up for perhaps the greatest of all the creative achievements of Cranmer, his English Prayer Book. He seems to have presented a first draft of the first book to two meetings of bishops at the end of 1548. It was, of course, a compromise. As far as possible the medieval order and ceremonies were retained, but there was a good deal of simplification, a more prominent place was given to edification, and the grosser doctrinal implications were avoided although not perhaps deliberately negated. Effectively sponsored by Cranmer and Ridley,[48] the proposals were carried in Convocation and the Lords, but before the bill became law there had to be modifications in a more conservative direction.[49] Still, Cranmer had attained his main objective. He had given to the nation a worthy instrument of public worship in the language of the people.

Rather surprisingly, perhaps, the book did not have too good a reception. The extremists disliked it because it was too conservative,[50] the traditionalists because it was too advanced, and the ordinary people because it was new. The Prayer Book was a definite contributory factor to the south-western revolt

---

47. P.S., II, p. 430 f.
48. Cf. *Original Letters*, II, pp. 469-470.
49. *Original Letters*, I, p. 323.
50. *Original Letters*, I, pp. 232-233, 323, 251.

of the same year, and although the main grievances were certainly economic, the religious aspect cannot be ignored. Of course, many of the Cornish did not understand English anyway, so that the book was of no great value to them, but the main resistance was simply to change. Cranmer did not find it very difficult to expose the ignorance and illogicality and even irreligion of some of the objections,[51] but the fact remained that time would be needed before his work would establish itself in the minds and hearts of the people.

More galling, however, than all the criticism was the claim of Stephen Gardiner that he could find his doctrine of the real presence in the new communion office. This, perhaps, more than any other factor made revision inevitable and determined its character. It had the more immediate consequence of plunging the archbishop into the controversial writing and disputation which in fair weather and foul occupied Him for the remaining years of his life. To his *True and Catholic Doctrine of the Lord's Supper* Gardiner and Smith made rejoinders which Cranmer had to refute in his *Answer*, and when Gardiner replied again he spent his last months in prison composing a fresh defence which has not survived.[52] These writings on the eucharist are Cranmer's only detailed and systematic contribution to technical theology.

Doctrinally, the south-western rebellion was of no serious consequence, but economically and politically it had critical results. There were similar risings in other parts of the country and attention was focused on the gross mismanagement of the régime. Somerset's attempts at redress only alienated his fellow-nobles. In addition, troops had to be withdrawn from Scotland and France to crush the insurgents at home, and this led to reverses which further discredited the government. The Duke of Northumberland, who largely put down the revolts, profited by the situation to combine all the discontented elements against Somerset, and the latter had no option but to accept the mediation of Cranmer and surrender to his opponent. Cranmer has been blamed sometimes for his part in the *coup d'état*, but he was assured that Somerset would not suffer in

---

51. P.S., II, pp. 163 f.   52. P.S., II, pp. 455-456.

Introduction: The Reformer

person, property or dignity, and he could not foresee his later imprisonment, attainder and execution.

All the same, Cranmer must have had serious misgivings when Somerset was succeeded by Northumberland. He had worked well with the former, but he had no liking for the latter, whose ruthlessness and rapacity he clearly discerned.[53] Indeed, at first, he did not even know that Northumberland would favour the Reformation.[54] Like many plotters, Northumberland had held out conflicting promises to different factions. He did not declare his hand until he had first secured his own position. The choice then fell on the reforming side, but it was a choice of self-interest and not of conviction. Cranmer for one saw this clearly. He could never think of Northumberland as "a most holy and fearless instrument of the Word of God"[55] as did some of the extremists whom the Duke encouraged.[56] In consequence, the short period of Northumberland's supremacy was for Cranmer an uneasy and unhappy time when he was continually in opposition and had to shape hostile forces and circumstances to a pattern of ultimate spiritual enrichment.

One of the first acts of the new government was the appointment of a commission to draw up a new ordinal. Cranmer seems to have played a leading part in the revision, which completed the first instalment of liturgical reform. The ancient service was drastically purged and simplified. Only the three main orders were now recognized. Episcopal ordination remained, but there was a new insistence on divine calling, popular assent and the ministry of word and sacrament. Sacerdotal ideas were carefully excluded, and the service was not based on the presupposition that orders are themselves a sacrament. To the reactionaries the new ordinal was thoroughly distasteful, but the retention of vestments and the oath by the saints proved a stumbling-block to radicals like Hooper.[57] In fact, it was from the ordinal that the Puritan controversies had their first beginning, for at Easter, 1550, Hooper was appointed to the vacant bishopric of Gloucester,[58] and he tried to persuade the King and Council to waive the authorized forms in his

---

53. Cf. P.S., II, p. 444.   54. Cf. *Original Letters*, I, p. 70.
55. *Ibid.*, p. 89.   56. *Ibid.*, p. 83.   57. *Ibid.*, p. 81.   58. *Ibid.*, p. 87.

case.⁵⁹ But Cranmer and Ridley,⁶⁰ assisted by Bucer and Martyr,⁶¹ insisted upon proper obedience in a matter essentially indifferent, and they carried their point, although it was only after a short spell in the Fleet prison that Hooper submitted. The issue was trifling enough, like those which provoked the later controversies, but a great principle was ultimately at stake. Is the church committed in every detail to the precept and precedent of Scripture, or is there an area of things indifferent in which it is free to take order so long as it does not legislate against Scripture? Cranmer and Ridley were both of the latter view, which found its expression in the article (34), and its final defence in the detailed arguments of Whitgift and the masterly theses of Hooker.

In relation to the Hooper episode Cranmer carried his point, but when it came to the continued spoliation of church property his protests were unavailing against the greed of the nobility.⁶² There were many ways of plundering the church. Benefices could be left unfilled, or supplied by servants, and the temporalities appropriated by patrons. Valuable ornaments could be removed on the pretence of reformation. Scholarships could be claimed for the wealthy. On an even bigger scale, the remaining chantry endowments were a rich prize. Manors could be extorted on the appointment of bishops. Bishoprics could be suppressed or their endowments taken over in return for a fixed stipend. Against all these abuses Cranmer and Ridley and Latimer and later Knox and Hooper maintained a constant opposition. Where genuine reform made necessary a re-application of endowments, as in the case of the chantries, they attempted to secure the money for religious, educational and charitable projects.⁶³ But their efforts were only partially successful and a source of irritation to the despoilers. The climax came in the last months of the régime when Tunstall of Durham was deprived and there was a scheme to reorganize his wealthy bishopric. Cranmer resisted the deposition,⁶⁴ and if Ridley had been appointed as suggested it is likely that there

---

59. *Original Letters*, II, p. 567.
60. Ibid., pp. 486-487.
61. Ibid., p. 494.
62. Cf. Ridley (P.S.), pp. 59, 410-411.
63. Cf. *Narratives of the Reformation*, p. 247.
64. Pollard, *op. cit.*, p. 260.

Introduction: The Reformer

would have been a headlong collision over the projected reorganization.

Still, the rapacity of the nobles made possible the deeper and more permanent reforms which Cranmer himself desired, and as in the reign of Henry he profited by the situation to do a less obvious but in the long run more decisive work. It was not entirely of his own choosing. If Cranmer had had his way, reforms would have come more slowly, prepared by a more thorough indoctrination by the Word of God. But Cranmer did not know, of course, how short was the time available. As it turned out, it was as well for the church, or at any rate for the reformation of the church, that the archbishop was hustled by events. The work done was superficial and transitory as he himself saw it, but it formed a solid basis for the more enduring settlement of the Elizabethan period.

Prayer Book revision was the first item in the programme. Many circumstances combined to make this desirable. The 1549 book had never become popular. The extremists in particular wanted something more definite and radical. Individual action, as for example Ridley's replacement of altars by communion tables,[65] had altered the emphasis and even the ethos of worship. The criticisms of Martyr and the detailed suggestions of Bucer underlined the need for reform. Above all, it was realized that the first version still left a loop-hole for the traditionalists. This perhaps more than any other factor inclined Cranmer to accept the principle of revision, and in January, 1552, the second Book of Common Prayer was enforced by a new act of uniformity.

In every way it was more radical than its predecessor.[66] The old vestments and ornaments were abandoned. Ancient ceremonies were discontinued. A penitential introduction replaced auricular confession. In baptism, the water was no longer consecrated and trine immersion gave way to single. In communion, the canon of the mass was ruthlessly but imaginatively dismembered, and every suggestion of a substantial presence was scrupulously removed. To make doubly

---

65. Ridley (P.S.), pp. 319 f.
66. For a detailed comparison, cf. Liturgies of Edward VI (P.S.).

sure, Knox tried to persuade the Council to prevent kneeling reception. Cranmer and Ridley resisted this demand, but they added the explanatory rubric which explains that no adoration is intended to Christ corporally present. The book went through several editions in its short period of use, and if it was not practised long enough to exercise its full influence, it had a decisive importance as the basis of the 1559 and 1662 books.

The next item was the long projected revision of the canon law, for which a commission had been appointed in 1549. The sweeping changes of the last twenty years had made this reform imperative, for many canonical provisions were now contrary to statute law, and others had become obsolete or inoperative.[67] In addition, Cranmer saw the need for clear disciplinary provisions, and he wanted to bring canon law into line with the new liturgical and doctrinal standards. But the project was not a popular one, for the lay lords and especially Northumberland had no desire to bring themselves under the clear-cut discipline of the church. A system of confused and in many ways convenient law was in every way preferable, for in effect it meant very little law at all so far as they themselves were concerned. As it turned out, the commission appointed in 1549 did not receive authority to proceed until 1552, and since it had been appointed for only three years it failed to complete its work in time. This was the kind of obstruction which Cranmer had always encountered on this issue. The need for revision was unquestionable, but in fact no one wanted it. Cranmer did not despair. He brought to completion his projected *Reformatio Legum Ecclesiasticarum*, and although he was never able to submit it either to Convocation or Parliament it is an interesting testimony to his work. As in all such codes, the detailed provisions have dated, and we may be grateful that they do not have statutory authority. But taken as a whole, the scheme has the merit of conciseness and lucidity, and one at least of the suggestions, the revival of diocesan synods with lay representation, was of great constructive importance.

The third item was the introduction of a common doctrinal

---

67. Pollard, *op. cit.*, p. 280 n. 3; cf. P.S., II, pp. 68 f.

confession, and in this field Cranmer was much more successful. His aim was not to stifle private opinion, but to enforce an authoritative standard of teaching on controverted issues. In a sense, the *King's Book* did to some extent provide this standard, but the church had moved a good way since its publication and Cranmer himself had never been really satisfied with the book. On the other hand, the free proclamation of wildly conflicting opinions could only do harm, and as early as 1549 Cranmer drew up some articles for use in his own diocese. The success of the scheme prompted him to submit these or similar articles to his fellow-bishops in 1551 and then, through Cheke and Cecil,[68] to the King and Council in 1552. As finally amended, these articles were finally published as the Forty-Two Articles of June, 1553. They came too late to be of any practical value, but they have an obvious importance as the basis of the Thirty-Nine Articles finally adopted by both Convocation and Parliament during the reign of Elizabeth. In the sense that doctrines were not too narrowly defined, the aim of the articles was comprehension rather than exclusion. As far as practicable, Cranmer wanted to carry the whole church with him in religious "concord and quietness."[69] But the comprehensiveness must not be exaggerated, for traditionalist teaching is plainly rejected at the one end of the scale, and anabaptist at the other. It is apparent that Cranmer did not want either a detailed definition or a rigid enslavement of private opinion. But it is equally apparent that he had turned the authoritative doctrine of the church in an unmistakably reformed direction.

With the introduction of the articles Cranmer completed the threefold contribution – Bible, Prayer Book and Confession – which more perhaps than the political enactments of King and Council has revolutionized the church and nation. He was only just in time, for on July 6 Edward died, and after the futile conspiracy of Northumberland Mary's accession brought speedy ruin to these painful accomplishments. For the next two and a half years Cranmer had to endure the distressing spectacle of his life's work undone, his doctrines attacked, his

---

68. P.S., II, pp. 439-440.   69. P.S., II, pp. 440-441.

friends tortured and executed. He himself was subjected to every kind of physical, mental and moral pressure, so that it was only through shame and weakness that at the last, on March 21, 1556, he witnessed a good confession, committing himself and his work to the resurrecting power of God.

The end is in a sense characteristic of the whole. From the human standpoint Cranmer's work had always been in frailty and it concluded in apparent failure. He had never been entirely the master of either events or circumstances. For the most part he had had to work with rulers whom he found it impossible to oppose and difficult to advise or control. He was hampered in a way by his own conscientious acceptance of the royal supremacy, which brought him at the last almost to a betrayal of his deepest convictions. But in and through it all he had accomplished an inward reformation of piety, worship and doctrine, which was not merely a complement of the external work of government, but something which a wider and therefore a truer perspective has shown to be more basic and enduring.

1
The Scholar

From the time that he left Cambridge Cranmer was necessarily entangled in a good deal of administrative activity. He had his wider responsibilities as a member of the Council and a leader in Convocation and the House of Lords. He also had the not inconsiderable day to day business of his own diocese and household. In the circumstances it is not surprising that he made no very direct or more strictly academic contribution to theological scholarship, or that his attainments as a scholar could be almost forgotten by his younger contemporaries. Indeed, the ability with which he espoused the 1549 Prayer Book came as something of a surprise to the new generation: "The palm rests with our friends, but especially with the Archbishop of Canterbury, whom they till now were wont to traduce as a man ignorant of theology, and as being conversant only with matters of government."[1] It has to be remembered, of course, that those who had put out this opinion were his ecclesiastical opponents, and at bottom it was a rejection of his theology rather than a criticism of his attainments. Vilification is often a more potent weapon than argument. On the other hand, even the more militant reforming group expressed their impatience in a similar way when Cranmer translated the catechism of Justus Jonas: "This Thomas hath fallen into so heavy a slumber that we entertain but a very cold hope that he will be aroused even by your most learned letter."[2] In other words, if Cranmer had been a sound and alert theologian he would obviously have held the same views as we do.

Of course, after twenty years' absence from the direct life of the schools it was hardly surprising that the earlier academic record should have been forgotten or that Cranmer should be regarded as a back number. Yet in his own day Cranmer had certainly been one of the ablest and most promising of the

---

1. *Original Letters*, II, pp. 469-470.   2. *Ibid.*, pp. 380-381.

younger Cambridge theologians. His college had thought sufficiently highly of his attainments not only to give him a fellowship but to recall him to it after the death of his first wife, although normally the statutes were interpreted to exclude widowers as well as married men. During the years which followed he had not only proceeded to his doctorate but had become an examiner in the theological faculty. He did not have the means or influence to move quickly to high honour or distinction, but he was obviously making his way by solid merit and achievement, and Wolsey would have liked him for his new foundation at Oxford. Against the twenty years of administration we have to balance the twenty years of theological scholarship which preceded them. And we have to remember that the years devoted to theology were the most active and the most formative.

A further point is that Cranmer's methods of study were calculated to stand him in good stead when he did not have the same leisure for detailed reading. By the standards of his day he was always an omnivorous reader. He amassed a private library which was larger than the whole university library of his undergraduate days, although of course we must not forget that printing was a comparatively recent invention and the rapid multiplication of books was only just beginning in the early sixteenth century. In addition to the Greek New Testament and two Hebrew Bibles Cranmer's collection contained a fairly complete set of the fathers, many of the school-men, and all the leading writers of his own century. He seems to have read slowly, but he had the habit of careful annotation, for "he seldom read without pen in hand, and whatsoever made either for the one part or the other of things being in controversy, he wrote it out if it were short, or, at the least, noted the author and the place, that he might find it, and write it out by leisure"[3] By this means he gathered a large store of readily accessible knowledge which enabled him to weigh every side of a controverted issue and to come always to an informed and responsible judgment.

But even in his years as archbishop Cranmer did not rely

---

3. *Narratives of the Reformation*, p. 219.

The Scholar

only on his past acquisition of knowledge. His opportunities for reading were more limited, but by a methodical arrangement of his daily time-table he made the most of the time available. If Foxe's account is correct,[4] he normally devoted the first four hours of every day, from 5 o'clock to 9, to prayer and reading. After that, he committed the business of the day to the various officers of his household, and then whenever possible "associated with learned men, for the sifting and boulting out one matter or another". The afternoon and evening were often claimed for outside business, but any time that could be spared was given to reading and discussion, so that the habits formed at Cambridge were carried forward into the new and very different circumstances.

Indeed, in spite of the greater distractions, Cranmer had certain advantages in the new life. On the purely mechanical side, he now had the assistance of a secretary, so that he could continue his method of annotation with greater speed and less drudgery. The latter common-place books have come down to us and can be consulted in the British Museum. They are in the hand of Cranmer's secretary Morice, with various notes made directly by Cranmer himself. They give clear evidence not only of the methodical nature but also of the breadth and depth of Cranmer's reading even during his tenure of the archbishopric. There is also the further point that his contacts widened considerably with his advancement. In Cambridge, it is true, he had had the society of scholars and the assistance of books and a bookish atmosphere. But at Lambeth he was in constant touch with some of the best minds of the age, and he entered into direct communication with many of the leading continental scholars. During the reign of Edward especially, Lambeth became a kind of clearing-house of theologians and theological discussion, and Cranmer's own thinking took on a new liveliness and conviction. It was also his duty as archbishop to be a patron of younger scholars. Ridley in particular was a protégé of Cranmer, but so too were Bradford, Grindal, Jewel[5] and Parker.[6] In many respects Cranmer was the giver

---

4. P.S., I, p. xi.
5. His final letter to Peter Martyr is thought to have been taken by Jewel. Cf. P.S., II, p. 457.
6. Cf. P.S., II, pp. 418, 425.

in this relationship, and the later Elizabethan leaders all show clear evidence of Cranmer's influence. On the other hand, the traffic was not all one way. Ridley in particular exercised a strong and on the whole perhaps beneficial influence on his more cautious if no less erudite colleague and patron, and the younger men generally helped to keep him open and alert in his thinking and approach.

The testimony of those who knew Cranmer is interesting if not altogether consistent. On the one side, it seemed to be a settled policy of his opponents to decry the scholarship of the archbishop. This emerges very clearly in the reply of Stephen Gardiner, who time and again suggests that there is nothing original in his work, but that he is deriving his ideas and arguments from Peter Martyr: "He doth but as it were translate Peter Martyr, saving he roveth at solutions, as liketh his phantasy".[7] It is also emphasized in the examination, when he is accused of a feeble vacillation in the matter of the eucharist, and Ridley is charged with the main responsibility for Edwardian teaching.[8] In the case of Gardiner, it seems evident that there was a good deal of personal animosity. By a mere stroke of fate his less prominent Cambridge contemporary had suddenly outstripped him in honour and influence. But on the traditionalist side generally it was easier to discount Cranmer as an ignoramus than to give a solid answer to his teaching.

As against the denigration of opponents, the opinion of Henry VIII is useful and not altogether irrelevant. Henry had a considerable taste for theology – more, perhaps, than he had for ethics. He enjoyed theological disputation, and could take part in it with unruffled patience and temper. For his own part, he inclined strongly to traditionalist positions, but he was never a bigot in controversy, and if he enforced external uniformity he welcomed the interplay of private opinions. On disputed issues he seems to have leaned heavily on Cranmer's learning, even though he did not always follow his judgment: "At all times when the King's Majesty would be resolved in

---

7. P.S., I, p. 195.
8. P.S., II, pp. 217-218; but cf. the tribute of Ridley (P.S.), p. 161.

any doubt or question, he would but send word to my Lord overnight, and by the next day the King should have in writing brief notes of the doctors' minds, with a conclusion of his own mind, which he could never get in such readiness of none, no, not of all his clergy and chaplains about him, in so short a time."[9] This quotation is very revealing. It not only displays the confidence of the King. It also shows us that Cranmer's judgments were based always on a solid foundation of knowledge, and that if he sometimes hesitated, it was not because of weakness but because of his grasp and appreciation of more than one side of a question. In our own day as in Cranmer's the greatest cocksureness is often a mask for the profoundest ignorance. A bold novelty is easy when the lessons of the past are not known. The originality of idea or utterance has to replace a solidity of learning and information. Set in the light of past discussion the novelty is soon shown to be superficial. Henry, at any rate, recognized the genuine scholarship of the archbishop. As he is once said to have put it to Stephen Gardiner when they were arguing a question with Cranmer: "My Lord of Canterbury is too old a truant for us twain."[10]

The learning of Cranmer was also appreciated by his contemporaries abroad. In some cases the tributes paid were merely conventional, as when Erasmus referred to him as "a most upright man of spotless life". In letters from Bucer, Bullinger and Calvin we find similar protestations of respect,[11] but these can hardly be accepted as solid evidence. Again, when Bucer and Fagius were enjoying the hospitality of Lambeth and dependent upon the protection of the archbishop it is hardly surprising that they should describe him as "that most benevolent and kind father of the churches and of godly men".[12] The scholar who had the highest opinion of Cranmer, and who probably knew him best, was Peter Martyr. Like Cranmer, Martyr was very well versed in the fathers, and his cast of mind and thought seems to have been very similar to that of the

---

9. *Narratives of the Reformation*, p. 249.
10. *Ibid.*, p. 250.
11. Cf. *Original Letters*, II, p. 711.
12. *Ibid.*, p. 535.

archbishop. He obviously had a very great admiration for Cranmer: "But now, believe me, he has shown himself so mighty a theologian against them, as they would rather not have proof of, and they are compelled, against their inclination, to acknowledge his learning, and power and dexterity in debate."[13] Martyr, of course, seems to have had a thorough understanding of the difficulties which faced the archbishop, so that he could not approve the impatient criticisms of those extremer foreigners who boosted Hooper as their English champion. His letters refer constantly to the bitterness of the opposition: "The perverseness of the bishops is incredible; they oppose us with all their might." But the weight of hostility only enhances the pertinacity of the archbishop: "The labour of the most reverend the archbishop of Canterbury is not to be expressed. For whatever has hitherto been wrested from we have acquired solely by the industry, and activity, and importunity of this prelate."[14] For Martyr Cranmer was a "standard-bearer" among the bishops "not ill-inclined" to reform.[15] The general impression from Martyr's letters is one of a deep sympathy and understanding which inspired a high admiration for Cranmer's endowment and tenacity. He was able to inspire his pupils with something of the same enthusiasm, for at first John ab Ulmis had been a severe critic of the archbishop,[16] but he later wrote: "The Archbishop of Canterbury, a man of singular worth and learning, has contrary to the general expectation, delivered his opinion upon this subject learnedly, correctly, orderly, and clearly; and by the weight of his character, and the dignity of his language and sentiments, easily drew over all his hearers to our way of thinking."[17] But perhaps by this time ab Ulmis realized that Martyr and Cranmer stood for what was substantially his own position.

One thing is clear. Cranmer did not make any very considerable contribution in theological writing. When we survey even his total literary remains, it is astonishing how small is the quantity compared with the vast bulk of Luther or Calvin

---

13. *Ibid.*, p. 470.
14. *Ibid.*, p. 480.
15. *Ibid.*, p. 482.
16. *Ibid.*, pp. 380-381.
17. *Ibid.*, p. 388.

or the lesser but impressive tomes of Zwingli. It is true, of course, that the two volumes of the Parker Society edition are both substantial and run to several hundred pages. But when we examine them, we find that there is not a great deal of direct theology. The main treatise is the *True and Catholic Doctrine* and the more detailed and scattered *Defence*, which together comprise the first volume. There is also a work on Scripture and Tradition, although this seems to have been put together and augmented by a Marian editor. For the rest we are dependent upon various papers and fragments and writings which are only indirectly theological. The preoccupation with ecclesiastical business is no doubt responsible in the main for this paucity of theological utterance. But there may be, perhaps, another and a deeper reason. The temperament of Cranmer was more that of the pure scholar than the independent thinker. His primary impulse was to amass knowledge rather than to state or discuss it.

Yet that is not the whole truth, for Cranmer is responsible for a tremendous amount of what we are forced to describe as indirect theology. For example, he had a hand in several confessions of faith, from the Ten Articles of 1536 to the Forty-Two Articles of 1553. Again, he was interested in the successive statements of doctrine which were issued for instructional purposes: the *Bishops' Book*, the *King's Book*, *Cranmer's Catechism* and possibly the Catechism issued with the Forty-Two Articles and usually ascribed to Ponet. We have to be careful, of course, that we do not appeal too confidently to these writings as an expression of Cranmer's own opinions, for there is no doubt that he did not like the *King's Book*, and it is doubtful whether he was really satisfied with its predecessor. More important from this standpoint is the first book of *Homilies* issued early in the reign of Edward, for Cranmer has always been regarded as the author of the great series on justification to which there is still a reference in the article (11). By their very nature the *Homilies* have a pronounced homiletical tendency, but all the same they have a definite doctrinal importance and Cranmer had a fairly free hand in their composition.

Even the Prayer Books are theological in an indirect sense,

for at the most important points the changes in the form and structure of worship were determined on dogmatic rather than strictly liturgical grounds. This was particularly true in the case of the communion service, but in varying degrees it is true of all the services. The consecration of the baptismal water was not omitted merely because it is a dispensable ceremony, but because of underlying dogmatic implications. Similarly, prayers for the dead have to be excluded to safeguard a true doctrine of redemption by Jesus Christ, and the introduction of a general confession instead of the "sacrament" of penance is governed entirely by dogmatic and not liturgical considerations. It is for this reason that the Prayer Book is so often regarded, and with partial justification, as a supplementary confession of faith. We have to be careful, of course, not to read the liturgies merely as doctrinal statements. Obviously the language of piety cannot have the same precision as that of dogmatics, and the former ought to be interpreted in terms of the latter rather than *vice versa*. From 1549 to the present day the Church of England has suffered from an inveterate and apparently ineradicable tendency to treat the Prayer Book as a primary and even an autonomous confessional utterance. On the other hand, there is an evident inter-action, which Cranmer himself realized, between liturgy and doctrine, and from first to last the revision of the services, like every achievement of Cranmer, was regarded as a theological task.

Indeed, the more closely we consider his work, the more we see that it was dominated by a theological aim and method. He had no primary interest in the practical reformation of the church, which he was content for the most part to leave to the civil authorities. The concern of the archbishop was not merely that this or that abuse should be remedied or arrangement improved. It went a good deal deeper. It was a concern that the medieval system as a whole should give way to a reformed and therefore as he saw it a scriptural and a truly catholic system. To accomplish this task all sorts of practical measures had to be taken and Cranmer was ready to bring such pressure as he could where something vital was at stake. But his own positive contribution was primarily in the less tangible field of the word and sacrament. He gave to his church a Bible, biblical preaching, a catechism, a Prayer Book and a confession of faith. If he has nothing much to offer in the way of dogmatic treatises, the reforms for which he himself was in the main responsible are all at the theological level.

But he also had a theological strategy, for like Luther himself he believed and foresaw that this deeper reformation by the word would issue in a more thorough-going reformation of practice and conduct. Of course, Cranmer was far too much of a theologian to regard doctrinal preaching and instruction merely as the means to a practical or ecclesiastical end. It is a primary aim in itself. But he was also far too much of a theologian to think that the theological or religious world is an isolated one which does not have a very profound effect on affairs in general. If the people could be systematically indoctrinated in evangelical truth, the more mundane problems of the church and nation would necessarily solve themselves. It was for this reason, or better perhaps, with this necessary byproduct also in view, that Cranmer concentrated upon the preaching and teaching of the Gospel, disseminating the Scriptures, introducing exhortations into all possible services, insisting upon instruction in the Creed, Lord's Prayer and Ten Commandments, ordering the preaching of sermons or homilies, publishing catechisms and taking care for the proclamation of sound scriptural and catholic doctrine. The attempted development of schools and colleges was also an integral part of the basic strategic programme.

In two respects, it may be, Cranmer miscalculated. For one thing, he thought of his own task rather too narrowly as theological, leaving the more practical arrangements much too readily to the civil powers. Theoretically, of course, the proclamation of the word was to influence and inspire the civil rulers, but in practice it did not altogether work out that way, and in England as in Lutheran Germany the thoroughgoing reformation by the Word of God was never accomplished. Far too often the arrangements which were left to the civil powers were determined by purely practical or even selfish rather than theological or spiritual factors, and Cranmer's sharp separation of spiritual and temporal functions proved an obstacle rather than a help to his own ultimate objective. At this point Zwingli and Calvin saw deeper than Luther and Cranmer, for they realized that theological responsibility does not cease with proclamation and instruction, but has to see to a practical outworking in the life of church and nation.

But second, Cranmer had not reckoned on the fact that even the theological programme could not be carried out properly without practical measures of ecclesiastical reform. It is one thing to insist on a definite policy of preaching and teaching, but this policy can be put into effect only if there is a properly qualified, deployed and disciplined ministry. In sixteenth-century England this meant that there would have to be more and better schools and a thorough reorganization of diocesan and parochial life. The vast endowments of monasteries and chantries could have supplied this need and Cranmer and his fellow-reformers did their best to secure as much of the endowments as possible for educational and ecclesiastical projects. But for the most part their efforts were unsuccessful, and the failure in practical reform meant inevitably a partial failure in the theological. Because of the practical breakdown there was cumulative obstruction where there might otherwise have been cumulative development. The circle of inter-action was turning the wrong way.

The fact remains, however, that by impulse, aim and strategy, Cranmer worked as a theologian rather than an administrator, and that in spite of every obstacle he achieved a fair measure of success even in his own century, quite apart from the almost incalculable influence of his work on the centuries which followed. It is the theological character of his activity which makes it so difficult to form an impartial judgment of Cranmer. If we try to assess him by administrative standards, we shall be tempted to write him off as almost a complete failure: which would, of course, be quite unjust. Again, if we do not share or at least understand his theological outlook and teaching, his achievements will be real enough but distasteful or even disastrous. Because he operated at the deep level of the Word and the Spirit, Cranmer's greatness has necessarily an enigmatic quality, which is also apostolic. His weapons were not carnal, but mighty through God to the pulling down of strongholds. His accomplishments were not the striking successes of administration, but the unnoticed, intangible, incalculable things which in the long run have often the most decisive and enduring consequences.

2
Scripture and Tradition

With Cranmer, as with Luther and Zwingli, the first and liberating change came in the attitude and approach to the Bible. For this, Cranmer seems in the first instance to have been indebted to humanistic influences. He was nurtured in the old learning, but his years in Cambridge coincided with the influx of new ideas under the stimulating direction of Fisher. The earlier opposition of the Friars was gradually overcome. Greek was introduced into the university curriculum. A preachership was established for sermons in English. A new interest began to be felt in the actual text of Scripture, and Erasmus himself spent a short period as a lecturer in Queens. The result of all this activity was to send Cranmer back from the school-men to the Latin and even to the Greek fathers. But he could not stop there, and his ultimate goal was the actual text of the Bible itself.

The decisive year for Cranmer seems to have been 1516-17, when Luther was flinging out his challenge and Erasmus published his Greek Testament. According to his biographer, it was at this period that he commenced a systematic rethinking of controverted issues in the light of the Bible's own teaching: "Then he, considering what great controversy was in matters of religion (not only in trifles, but in the chiefest articles of our salvation), bent himself to try out the truth herein; and, forasmuch as he perceived that he could not judge indifferently in so weighty matters without the knowledge of the. Holy Scriptures (before he were infected with any man's opinions or errors), he applied his whole study three years to the said Scriptures."[1] In this shift in scholastic emphasis three important factors were involved. First, Cranmer turned to the original Greek and Hebrew so far as the then manuscripts allowed. Second, he tried to penetrate to the actual teaching

---

1. *Narratives of the Reformation*, p. 219.

of the text apart from the successive layers of patristic and scholastic commentary. And third, he followed the humanist principle and took the Bible only in its primary and literal sense and not in a secondary and allegorical.

The revolution had a direct influence upon the university and university teaching, for when he was examiner in the divinity school Cranmer expected from his candidates a firsthand knowledge of the biblical text. "Now doctor Cranmer, ever much favouring the knowledge of the scripture, would never admit any to proceed in divinity, unless they were substantially seen in the story of the bible: by means whereof certain friars and other religious persons, who were principally brought up in the study of the school-authors, without regard had to the authority of scriptures, were commonly rejected by him; so that he was greatly for that his severe examination of the religious sort much hated and had in great indignation: and yet it came to pass in the end, that divers of them, being thus compelled to study the scriptures, became afterwards very well learned and well affected; insomuch that, when they proceeded doctors of divinity, they could not overmuch extol and commend master doctor Cranmer's goodness towards them, who had for a time put them back to aspire unto better knowledge and perfection."[2] But it had an even greater influence on Cranmer's own thinking, for it meant his acceptance of the ultimate superiority of Holy Scripture over all other authorities. We cannot say, of course, that at this stage Cranmer had worked out the implications in detail. Both now and later he preserved a very high respect for the catholic authority of the fathers and the early creeds and councils. But there is no doubt that the plain text of the Bible had now become for him the only autonomous or conclusive authority.

The application of this principle can be seen first in Cranmer's attitude to the so-called divorce, and the whole complex of related problems. As he himself viewed it, the marriage of Henry was void from the very first because it contravened the plain law of Leviticus. Of course, the church and its rulers have a definite right to make or even to alter laws in matters

---

2. P.S., I, p. viii.

which are not covered by the binding law of Scripture. For that reason matrimonial dispensation cannot be rejected out of hand. But neither the Papacy nor any other court can dispense from a clear scriptural injunction. The fact that this is unfortunate for Katherine or convenient for Henry does not affect the ultimate theological issue. Rather strangely, Cranmer does not seem to have considered the view apparently defended by Melanchthon, that the letter of Old Testament legislation does not apply except in moral cases.[3] Or possibly in the distinction between the moral and the ceremonial law he took it that matrimonial questions have always a moral character. But the main point is plain enough. In any conflict between the law and teaching of Scripture and the law and teaching of the church, precedence must always be given to the former. The far-reaching nature of this principle is easily seen when we consider how many of the later reforms, the marriage of clergy or the granting of the cup to the laity or even the attitude to pilgrimages or purgatory, derived from this source.[4]

The principle had another important consequence for Cranmer, for it led him to an investigation and rejection of the supposed prerogatives of the Papacy. Ultimately, this was perhaps the main concern of Cranmer in the divorce issue. It was not merely that the authority of the Papacy must be subjugated to that of Scripture. It had also to be questioned and negated by that of Scripture. The royal headship could be maintained because Scripture would "bear" it. It rested on the plain precedents of the Old Testament and the clear and indisputable teaching of the New. But for the papal headship there was only the flimsiest of biblical evidence. The ramifications of this question need not be pursued in the present context, although they were discussed by Cranmer in great detail. What is important is that both the divorce and the underlying issue of supremacy were submitted by Cranmer to the final arbitrament of Scripture.

During his years as archbishop, Cranmer never had the

---

3. Cf. *Original Letters*, II, p. 556, where the marriage seems to be classed as a "political matter".
4. P.S., II, p. 215.

opportunity to systematize his doctrine of the Bible. Apart from one main statement, to which we shall return in a moment, it is best seen in application rather than in theoretical formulation. This is not altogether surprising, for Cranmer was forced by circumstances to devote himself to definite practical issues rather than to abstract theorizing. A fine example of his method is in relation to disputed questions like confirmation and the private mass, in which his first appeal is always to the biblical text: "There is no place in scripture that declareth this sacrament to be instituted of Christ";[5] "I think it more agreeable to the scripture and primitive church, that the first usage should be restored again, that the people should receive the sacrament with the priest."[6] Sometimes even the form of the question shows the drift of Cranmer's thinking, for in relation to the sacraments and the number of sacraments he asks first: "What a sacrament is by the scripture?" and then: "What a sacrament is by the ancient authors?"[7] A more extended instance of the same method is to be found in the *True and Catholic Doctrine of the Lord's Supper*, in which the first concern of Cranmer is to establish a true doctrine of the eucharist from the relevant passages of Scripture.[8] Other examples could easily be adduced, and his whole encouragement of Bible translation and Bible reading is in line with the same conviction.

When we come to the more detailed statement, Cranmer's primary objective is to overthrow the rival authority of unwritten traditions. It is not likely that the *Confutation of Unwritten Verities*[9] was ever prepared for publication by Cranmer himself, and he is not responsible for the present arrangement or headings. On the other hand there seems to be little doubt that the anonymous editor has made use of material actually amassed by Cranmer.[10] We can ignore the preface and the concluding chapter, which were obviously written by the translator and redactor.[11] Apart from these, there are ten main chapters, and in different ways they are all designed to

---

5. P.S., II, p. 80.
6. P.S., II, p. 151.
7. P.S., II, p. 115.
8. P.S., I, pp. 23 f.
9. P.S., II, pp. 1 f.
10. Cf. Jenkins, IV, p. 144.
11. P.S., II, pp. 9-19, 62-67.

demonstrate that only those doctrines which have biblical sanction have to be believed in the church.

The first chapter is short but characteristic. It consists of the self-witness of the Bible to its own fundamental authority.[12] The second is very long,[13] and in a sense it is the most critical in the whole discussion. It consists of an appeal to the fathers for the purpose of delimiting their authority. Numerous passages are quoted from Irenaeus, Tertullian, Origen, Cyprian, Jerome, Athanasius, Basil and other fathers to show that they all accepted the binding and exclusive authority of the Bible. For good measure there are even citations from Anselm, Aquinas and Scotus. The argument is an interesting one and typical of the method of Cranmer as a well-versed patristic scholar. He did not intend, of course, that the authority of the Bible should be based finally upon that of the fathers, for that would involve a self-contradiction. Pride of place had already been given to the scriptural self-attestation. His aim rather was to turn upon his opponents their own weapons, accepting a certain authority of the fathers and the early church, but using it to confirm his own thesis of the primary authority of Scripture. It must be emphasized that the acceptance of patristic authority is not merely for the purposes of debate, but that Cranmer does in fact believe that his insistence on the authority of the Bible is itself the catholic and therefore the patristic doctrine.

From the third chapter to the seventh[14] Cranmer discusses the various possible foundations for unwritten in the sense of non-scriptural doctrine or customs. The legislative power of general councils is dismissed on the ground of citations from the fathers and the obviously non-obligatory nature of the rulings, many of which have in fact been flagrantly but not fatally disregarded.[15] He deploys texts from the Bible and numerous patristic judgments against the alternative sanctions of angelic oracles, apparitions from the dead, miracles and custom.[16] Rather strangely, Cranmer does not seem to have considered here the main traditionalist contention, that there

---

12. P.S., II, pp. 21-22.
13. P.S., II, pp. 22 f.
14. P.S., II, pp. 36-51.
15. P.S., II, pp. 36-37.
16. P.S., II, pp. 40 f.

is an oral apostolic tradition side by side with the written. Perhaps this theory had not yet attained its importance in the England of Cranmer's day. In the eighth chapter he completes the threefold argument which he again uses in the *True and Catholic Doctrine* and which seems to be characteristic of all his inquiries.

He has a brief appeal to reason, and some general arguments are advanced for the ultimate supremacy of the Bible.[17]

In the two final chapters Cranmer considers briefly some of the biblical and patristic texts commonly used by his opponents.[18] The ninth chapter is in many ways the most interesting of the whole work, for here at last Cranmer touches on the twofold question of a continuing work of the Holy Spirit and an oral tradition handed down from the disciples. His own interpretation is that the work of the Holy Spirit has reference only to the teaching which Christ Himself has already given. In the power of the Holy Spirit the necessary teaching of Christ is given permanent form in the evangelical records, and in the other apostolic writings an authoritative interpretation is given of the redemptive work of God in Jesus Christ. The subsequent and subjective work of the Holy Spirit in the church and in individual Christians is all in relation to this prior objectivization. If the apostles themselves gave instructions which never found their way into the New Testament, Cranmer explains that these relate only to "variable traditions, observations, ceremonies, and outward rites and bodily exercises, which must certainly be kept, but which the church has power to alter, replace, or suppress".[19] That which is indispensable to Christian faith and conduct has all been recorded in the scriptures of the Old and New Testament.

When we consider Cranmer's teaching, we are struck at once by his omissions. It is not surprising, perhaps, that he makes no effort to define the inspiration of Scripture, or its uniqueness as compared with other books. The pressing questions of our own age were not at issue in the time of Cranmer. But it was rather a different matter with the canon, for while the traditionalists defended the inclusion of the Old Testament

---

17. P.S., II, pp. 52-53.   18. P.S., II, pp. 53 f.   19. P.S., II, p. 55.

apocrypha, Luther went to the other extreme and regarded some of the New Testament writings with suspicion. Cranmer did not ignore this question altogether. He makes the two brief points, that "the primitive church of the apostles, and the oldest writers, and next to their time," approved the canon, but that the writings which they accepted were "no less true afore they were allowed by them, than since".[20] He also had a quotation from Cyprian which puts books like Ecclesiasticus in a special class as ecclesiastical, but does not grant them a genuine canonical status: "all which books (the fathers) would have to be read in the church, but not alleged as of authority to confirm any article of our faith."[21] But these are only incidental points, and there is no proper consideration of the problems raised.

As Cranmer sees it, the relationship between the Bible and the church is plain enough. The church cannot be described as mistress of Scripture merely by virtue of the fact that it is the human author and guardian. Only the first apostles were in fact the authors of Scripture and in matters of essential faith and conduct they wrote only as instructed by Christ Himself and inspired by the Holy Ghost. The present function of the church is to be the keeper of Holy Scripture, but only in the same way as the appropriate offices or officials are the custodians of public records. It has no more power than "the registers, recorders, stewards of courts, or town-clerks" or even judges, to "put to, or take away any thing from, the first original writings".[22] This means, of course, a complete subjection of the church to the Word of God, at any rate in the essential matters of faith and conduct. In the Bible God Himself has declared everything that is necessary to salvation and it is the function of the church to be taught by and to maintain the truth received in and through the witness to Jesus Christ. In support of this view Cranmer had several quotations from the fathers, as, for example, the sentence of Athanasius: "The holy scriptures, being inspired from God, are sufficient to all instruction of the truth."[23] He also pressed

---

20. P.S., II, p. 59.
21. P.S., II, p. 23.
22. P.S., II, p. 59.
23. P.S., II, p. 24.

the argument commonly used by the fathers, that to suspend truth on the decisions of the church is to introduce confusion by substituting a fallible and human authority for an infallible and divine.[24]

The peculiar method of Cranmer did not allow him to forestall the possible criticisms of this view. For that reason he may seem to be particularly vulnerable to those who do not share his presuppositions. But the following points must always be borne in mind in relation to his doctrine of a supreme scriptural authority. First, of course, he was not concerned in the least about the detailed inerrancy of the Bible from the standpoint of historical empiricism. Naturally, he regarded as the Bible as a reliable account of the facts. But Cranmer still preserved the theological as opposed to a historicist approach which does not accept empiricism as the gauge of ultimate truth. In his insistence on the primary and binding authority of the Bible his concern was for the Bible as God's Word, not for the Bible as a trustworthy source-book of Hebrew history.

But second, and along similar lines, Cranmer was not thinking of a possible substitute at the human level for the human authority of the Papacy. The Bible is not an authoritative book merely because of certain characteristics at the human level, that it is old, or of outstanding literary excellence, or historically inerrant. Nor in the last resort does it really resemble a public record which can be consulted legalistically. For the whole point about the Bible is not merely that it is the testimony of prophets and apostles, but that it is the Word of God Himself, and therefore itself, as inspired and used by the Holy Spirit, a living Word. The Bible is not authoritative because it is an ecclesiastical Magna Carta, and in that sense a paper pope. It is authoritative because it is the revelation of God Himself in the concrete attestation of Jesus Christ.

But cannot the same be said of the church or the ministry (and therefore perhaps the Papacy) in the sense that they too have the promised guidance of the Holy Spirit and the continuing task of the proclamation of Jesus Christ? Cranmer's third point is the good one that with all the reformers and surely

---

24. P.S., II, p. 52.

with the Bible itself he maintained a peculiar status of the apostles and the apostolic age. It is not merely that the apostles were the direct and chosen witnesses of God's ultimate revelation to man in the Word made flesh. It is also that they themselves had a particular endowment of the Holy Spirit for the primary task of witness. Certainly, the Holy Spirit is at work in the church and its teaching and ministry. But the Holy Spirit is at work now only upon the basis and with consistent reference to the work which He Himself has already done in Jesus Christ and the prophetic and apostolic witness to Jesus Christ embodied in the Scriptures. Sometimes a new formula may be required to make dogmatically explicit that which is implicit in the Bible. That is the possible justification of the Athanasian "of one substance". But true dogmatics will always be the exposition of that which is there rather than an imposition or even an evolving of something new. If there is a legitimate criticism of Cranmer, it is that he regarded the apostolic age rather naively as a golden time.[25] But he was right not to allow a philosophy of historical development to obscure the centrality of the incarnation and work of Christ, and therefore of the prophetic and apostolic testimony to that work.

In the essential questions of faith and conduct, the subjection of the church to the Bible was quite absolute. But as Cranmer saw it, there was no such absolute subjection in matters of ceremony and order. In this sphere the Bible had only what might be described as a negative rather than a positive function. It had been different, of course, in the Old Testament, but as the epistle to the Hebrews points out, the covenant of Sinai has now been superseded, and the New Testament does not lay down any alternative blue-print for church order. Questions of organization are to be decided by the church or the churches in accordance with changing conditions. The only restriction is that nothing must be done which is actually contrary to Scripture. But this rule is formulated in negative rather than positive terms, so that even practices which obtained in the New Testament are not necessarily to be

---

25. P.S., II, p. 514.

observed in the church or the churches to-day: "Yea, also the traditions, made by the apostles in full council at Jerusalem, may be, and already are taken away. ... And this of Paul, that a man should neither pray nor preach capped, or with his head covered, is also clean abolished."[26]

This teaching is a bold continuation into the New Testament of a distinction commonly accepted in relation to the Old. But it is not easy to see how exactly it can be justified in terms of Cranmer's own insistence upon the supremacy of Scripture. The abrogation of the ceremonial and presumably the civil law of the Old Testament is plainly taught in the New, but it is not so clear that the Bible allows us freely to set aside the precedents of the New, and there is the added difficulty that in so many cases, even in praying with the head covered or uncovered, the indifferent question of order is swallowed up in a by no means indifferent question of doctrine. The latter difficulty especially was acutely felt by Cranmer himself, for time and again in his liturgical revision he had to abolish an in itself unobjectionable ceremony, not because it was itself unscriptural, but because it necessarily implied an unscriptural doctrine. It is, of course, self-evident that the church has to have liberty to adapt itself to a changing external situation. No church can reproduce exactly the pattern of a New Testament congregation, because no church is now living in exact New Testament conditions. That is simple enough. What is not so simple is to fix the precise relationship between this obvious liberty and the accepted supremacy of Scripture. According to Cranmer, the relationship takes the form of a division of power. On the one side there is an area of things indifferent – what we might describe as the external or secular aspect of the church – and this is the territory in which liberty holds sway. On the other side, there is an area of doctrinal and ethical obligation – what we might call the inner or divine aspect of the church – and in this sphere we are bound to an absolute supremacy of Scripture. But it is doubtful whether this division can be carried through without some contradiction. For one thing, there is still a continual overlapping

---

26. P.S., II, p. 55.

of boundaries. Why should the church have authority to allow a man to pray covered, but not have authority to deny the cup to the laity or to suspend clerical marriage? Or again, what is the exact meaning of the constant limitation of the church's liberty by the proviso that it must not ordain anything contrary to Holy Scripture? It is one thing to allow an added ceremony, like the sign of the cross, but it is rather a different thing to suspend or alter something for which there is a plain precept or precedent in the New Testament. The principle for which Cranmer contends is clear and sensible enough, and it commended itself to the later Elizabethans in their tremendous battle with the Puritans. But in its detailed application it obviously needs to be thought through much more carefully than in the rather off-hand dicta of Cranmer.

An important aspect of Cranmer's doctrine is that in spite of the supreme authority which he ascribes to the Bible he still allows a firm subsidiary authority to the earlier fathers of the church. In his approach to all doctrinal questions Cranmer proceeds by the threefold rule of Scripture, fathers, and reason, in that order. He does not give to the fathers a primary or independent authority. The fact that a doctrine is patristic means that we have to give it very careful consideration, but it is no guarantee of its validity. It still has to be submitted to the test which the fathers themselves accept. Yet Cranmer has a very high regard for the fathers as the first interpreters of Scripture. He includes the early patristic period in the "golden time" of the church, for it was then that "blessed bishops, blessed priests, and other blessed persons of the clergy, received and proclaimed the scripture … and by preaching and teaching of these Testaments was the faith of Christ marvellously increased in many countries".[27]

The point of Cranmer's appeal to this subsidiary authority is very simple. He believed strongly that in contending for reforming doctrines he was not maintaining new truths, but those which were both apostolic and catholic. The innovations were all on the side of his opponents, who defended doctrines and practices for which there was no sanction either in the

---

27. P.S., II, p. 514.

Bible or in the first fathers. He put this plainly in his letter to Queen Mary when he spoke of the "best learned men reputed within this realm", some of whom favoured "the old, some the new learning, as they term it (where indeed that which they call the old is the new, and that which they call the new is indeed the old)".[28] Or again, in his eucharistic doctrine he expressed time and again his willingness to be judged by the old church, even to the point of saying that he would "gladly use the same words that they used, and not use any other words, but to set my hand to all and singular their speeches, phrases, ways, and forms of speech, which they do use in their treatises upon the sacrament, and to keep still their interpretation".[29] His complaint was that he was "accused for an heretic" only because he would not consent "to words not accustomed in scripture, and unknown to the ancient fathers, but newly invented and brought in by men",[30] and he was bold to maintain a challenge, later reissued and extended by Jewel, that "if they could bring forth but one old author, that saith in these two points as they say, I offered six or seven years ago, and do offer yet still, that I will give place unto them".[31] Even in his last confession he expressed his belief not only "in every article of the catholic faith, every clause, word, and sentence taught by our Saviour Jesus Christ, his apostles and prophets, in the new and old Testament", but also "in all articles explicate and set forth in the general councils".[32] The whole point of his earlier recantations, and the peculiar temptation to evasion implicit in them, was the statement that he "believed as the catholic church doth believe, and hath ever believed from the beginning of the catholic religion".[33]

We must emphasize again that in his appeal to the fathers Cranmer had no thought whatever of suspending either the truth or the true doctrine of the Bible on patristic sanction. On the contrary, he found in the fathers exactly the same view of Scripture as he found in Scripture itself. A true loyalty to the fathers involved a loyalty to the scriptures which they themselves exalted and by which they were content to be

---

28. P.S., II, p. 450.
29. P.S., II, p. 227.
30. *Loc. cit.*
31. P.S., II, p. 457.
32. P.S., II, p. 566.
33. P.S., II, p. 563.

judged. The patristic witness to the Bible had a particular importance for Cranmer, for in addition to confirming his own catholicity it fixed the true relationship and therefore the subordination of the fathers to Scripture. For that reason, Cranmer developed this theme in considerably greater detail than he did the biblical self-attestation. He exerted himself to give copious and conclusive proof that the fathers themselves had taught all that he himself taught in relation to the Bible. They had refused to give full canonical status to the Old Testament apocrypha.[34] They would not allow anything to be taught as necessary for which there was no scriptural sanction.[35] They had contended for the sole-sufficiency of the Bible.[36] They had subjected preaching to a biblical norm.[37] They had maintained the perspicuity of Scripture, and the rule that "testimonies of places being certain" should be followed "to take away the doubt of the uncertain sentences".[38] They had tested even the writings of other fathers by the scriptural rule: "For I do not account Cyprian's writings as canonical," as Augustine once wrote, "but weigh them by the canonical scriptures; and that in them which agreeth with canonical I allow to his praise; but that that agreeth not, by his favour I refuse."[39]

The self-subjection of the fathers to Scripture was of particular importance to Cranmer's own thinking. On the one hand, it preserved him from an uncritical enthusiasm for the fathers, as though any issue could be settled by a patristic tag irrespective of the Bible. On the other hand, it gave catholic authority to his primary contention, that the church and individual Christians are always under the judgment of Scripture, and therefore constantly under the possibility and indeed the necessity of reformation. Cranmer's own theology is perhaps an excellent illustration of this general rule. In no matter did he move easily from established positions. But because he was open and not closed to the reformative judgment of the Bible, he inclined steadily from his first convictions to what he saw to be more scriptural and catholic truth. The fathers helped

---

34. P.S., II, p. 23.
35. P.S., II, p. 22.
36. P.S., II, p. 24.
37. P.S., II, p. 25.
38. P.S., II, pp. 31-32.
39. P.S., II, p. 33.

him, not merely by their authority, but by the admitted limitation of their authority. Yet while Cranmer emphasized this limitation, he never became an individualist in the interpretation of Scripture, as though at a pinch he could always set his own reading of Scripture against all the fathers. He could grant that patristic utterances are dispensable and may even be wrong if they are not grounded in the Word of God. But against that he could also maintain that "every exposition of the scripture, whereinsoever the old, holy, and true church did agree, is necessary to be believed".[40]

For the most part in his work Cranmer identifies tradition with unwritten verities, that is to say, doctrines or practices handed down by word of mouth or by example. He does not dispute that many of these traditions may have the relative authority which can be conferred by the church itself. For instance, if certain vestments have commonly been worn, and they are not contrary to Scripture, and the church approves their continued use, then they ought to be received and respected by individuals. But this obviously meant a restriction of legitimate tradition to the area of things unnecessary to salvation and therefore to matters of order and ceremony. Against the argument that the Gospel itself was in the first instance an oral tradition, taught by Christ to the disciples and preached by the disciples to the world, Cranmer believed of course with all the reformers that his first tradition has now found written and therefore pure and reliable form in the apostolic records. For Cranmer, therefore, the New Testament is itself the essential apostolic tradition as opposed to the indifferent traditions of ceremony and organization. The one is invariable, because it belongs to the inward constitution of the church. The other is variable, because it belongs to the external and to some extent contingent expression. The one has been given a permanent and inviolable form. The other has the more flexible form of enactment and custom.

The merit of Cranmer's view is plain to see, and up to a point, of course, it was not denied even by his opponents. It is not in any sense a discovery of modern scholarship that the

---

40. P.S., II, p. 59.

New Testament embodies the oral proclamation of the apostolic church. Everyone could agree that the Gospel first handed down by word of mouth has now received in the New Testament a permanent form. Where the difference arose was in relation to the scope and sufficiency of that which is written. Is this the essential tradition in its entirety, or are there other beliefs and customs which have been communicated either openly or secretly from the first days, and are therefore no less obligatory than that which is written? Cranmer stood out rigidly for the former view, and in the light of medieval developments there can be little doubt that he was right. If the essential tradition is preserved in oral as well as written form, there can be no end to the possibilities of corruption, and in the long run that which is written will be so augmented or reinterpreted or even negated by that which is not, that confusion and falsehood will have undisputed sway in the church. The whole point of the New Testament is that under the Holy Spirit the original tradition of the apostles should be preserved in a pure and trustworthy form.

On the other hand it may be asked whether, in his anxiety to maintain this truth, Cranmer does not miss what we might call the true and positive element in the concept of an oral or vocal tradition. The fact remains that even though it has now been incorporated in the New Testament, in its first inception the Gospel was living proclamation. The fact also remains that to this very day, as Cranmer himself realized in his emphasis upon exhortation and preaching, the vocal proclamation of the word is complementary to the word written and a legitimate and indeed necessary part of the tradition. Operating against a false concept of tradition as something which supplements the written word, Cranmer did not see that the preaching which he himself favoured is itself a right and positive form of oral tradition. To pass on the faith it is not enough merely to hand down a collection of manuscripts or printed papers. The Gospel has to be proclaimed afresh in the living context of every age and situation. In that sense it is always oral or vocal tradition, although it is the apostolic tradition only in so far as it conforms to the apostolic norm and is therefore agreeable to Holy Scripture. Cranmer was right enough in his rejection of the medieval misunderstanding, but he was surely wrong in his confinement of tradition only to variable order and ceremonial. A positive doctrine of tradition as the living complement of Scripture in scriptural proclamation is the best and most effective antidote to the misinterpretation.

Of Cranmer, perhaps, more than some of the more vital thinkers of the Reformation we have to admit that his presentation of the doctrine of Scripture has very obviously dated. The reason for this is that it is so deliberately controversial in both aim and method. He is arguing all the time against the views in which he was nurtured and which were still strongly represented by his opponents. He has to take these views as he finds them and to give his answers accordingly. For an age which has different problems they do not always seem to be the right, or better, the relevant answers. Matters are emphasized which now seem to us to be of much smaller account. The things which interest us to-day are ignored or taken for granted. Yet within these limitations Cranmer does seem to have established one or two points or principles of rather more enduring value. Controversially, he makes good his contention that his own teaching is both scriptural and patristic. More positively, he gives a broad outline of that teaching which if in some respects it requires more detailed examination is not without its permanent relevance and validity. It is the same outline which emerges again in the more precise statements of the articles, which in their doctrine of Scripture and tradition bear clear marks of the inspiration and even the authorship of the archbishop.

3
Justification

The Scripture-principle is at the heart of all Cranmer's thinking, but we find the first, large-scale theological use in the sphere of justification. The primary challenge of Luther had been in this matter, so that no sixteenth-century theologian was able to escape it. There is no evidence that Cranmer himself was won either easily or quickly to a Lutheran understanding. But it is natural enough that this should be one of the principal points of Christianity which he reassessed in the light of his new study of the Bible. It is natural, too, that as a scholar he should try to bring to the Lutheran thesis an open and impartial mind, testing both the medieval and the contemporary statements by his own threefold standard of Scripture, the fathers and reason.

In point of fact we have an excellent example of the method of Cranmer in the *Notes on Justification* which have come down to us in manuscript and are reprinted in both the Jenkins and the Parker Society editions of Cranmer's works. For the most part these manuscripts are in Cranmer's own hand, and some of the passages are underscored in red ink, probably by Cranmer himself.[1] It is impossible to fix any very certain date. On the one hand, most of the later common-place books are in the hand of Cranmer's secretary, so that there is a strong presumption that they belong to an earlier period. On the other hand, the nature of the material suggests a period of definite conviction rather than mere inquiry, so that we cannot put them too soon. Obviously, however, the material collected in these pages is based on a thorough preliminary investigation.

The sub-title gives us a clue to the character of the *Notes*, for we are told that they are accompanied by "authorities from scripture, the fathers, and the schoolmen".[2] As a matter of fact, the notes properly speaking consist only of a few very

---

1. Jenkins, II, p. 121. 2. P.S., II, p. 203.

short propositions or conclusions, and at a generous estimate they can hardly constitute more than about one per cent of the whole. The rest of the work consists of quotations from the Bible, the fathers and the school-men in support of the primary theses. The scriptural appeal is primarily to the apostle Paul, but a good number of fathers are quoted, including Irenaeus, Origen, Basil, Ambrose, Jerome, Theodoret, Augustine and Chrysostom. The main scholastic witnesses are Peter Lombard, Thomas Aquinas, Anselm and Bernard.

The theses themselves are not without interest, for they set out in brief compass what Cranmer took to be the main points in a true doctrine of justification. He insisted, of course, that we must not on any account think of faith as a ground of justification, for ultimately justification is not even by faith but only by grace.[3] The doctrine of justification by faith was not designed in any sense to exalt faith as a chief or necessary work of man, but only to show the impossibility of justification except by the gracious work of God.[4] No human works can ever be sufficient to deserve remission of sin, but only Jesus Christ Himself.[5] In this matter of works Cranmer is clear in his own mind that Paul meant "all manner of works of the law, as well of the Ten Commandments, as of ceremonials arid judicials".[6] Many fathers had used the term "works" in the same comprehensive sense.[7] James did not mean to contradict Paul, but he referred to a justification which is "the declaration, continuation, and increase of that justification which Paul spake of before".[8] The primary concern in the doctrine of justification by faith was to emphasize that justification is only by Christ, and in that way to give glory only "to our Saviour Christ, which was offered upon the cross for our sins, and rose again for our justification".[9] Yet it is legitimate and necessary to say by faith only, because it is by faith that "we know God's mercy and grace promised by his word (and that freely for Christ's death and passion sake) and believe the same, and being truly penitent, we by faith receive the same".[10] The

---

3. P.S., II, p. 203.
4. P.S., II, p. 206.
5. P.S., II, pp. 207-208.
6. P.S., II, p. 209.
7. P.S., II, pp. 203, 206.
8. P.S., II, p. 207.
9. P.S., II, p. 208.
10. P.S., II, p. 210.

fact that we can do this only in faith means in effect that we transcribe the whole glory of our justification to the merits of Christ alone.[11]

In a very real sense, the later writings on justification were only an amplification of these primary but undeveloped propositions. For the most part they took a credal form, for the hand of Cranmer is plainly to be seen in the Ten Articles, the *Bishops' Book*, and especially the Forty-Two Articles. He did not have quite so much influence on the *King's Book*, but it is interesting that in his annotation of Henry's suggested revision of the *Bishops' Book* he introduced a fairly long and clear statement of his own doctrine of justification.[12] The primary genius of Cranmer seemed to be in the drafting of doctrinal and liturgical forms rather than in more expansive discussions. All the same, he did formulate his own views on justification in a very important contribution to the first book of *Homilies*, which was intended to have, a theological and not merely an exhortatory character. From a very early time the great *Homily of Salvation* and its attendants *Of the True, Lively, and Christian Faith*, and *Of Good Works*, have been ascribed to Cranmer, and this is supported by the patristic references, which are for the most part a selection of those found in the *Notes*. Gardiner himself described Cranmer as the author of the first of these homilies,[13] and his authorship of the whole trilogy is attested as early as 1567 in the *Christian Manual* of John Woolton, the nephew of Alexander Nowell the catechist.[14] There is therefore every reason to assume that these authoritative statements, to which there is an express reference in the present article 11, are a mature and careful expression of the teaching of Cranmer himself. Whether the article refers only to the first or comprehensively to the whole series is a debatable point. But theologically it is the first which is the most significant. The other two are written mainly with a view to pastoral application and instruction.

In the homilies, as in the *Notes* and article, the first and presumably the chief concern of Cranmer is to emphasize the

---

11. *Loc. cit.*
12. P.S., II, pp. 113-114.
13. P.S., II, p. 128 n. 1.
14. *Loc. cit.*

grace and glory of God as revealed in the person and work of Jesus Christ. He does not proclaim justification by faith in order to give prominence to faith or in any way to exalt it. What is recognized in this doctrine is that man cannot "by his own acts, words, and deeds (seem they never so good) be justified and made righteous before God".[15] For justification, he is wholly dependent upon "another righteousness, or justification", which he owes to the great mercy of God as expressed and realized in the atoning work of Jesus Christ, which is the conjunction of God's wrath and God's grace.[16] At the back of the insistence on faith there is a frank acknowledgment of the human situation as a hopeless one of sin and guilt and impotence. There is a clear apprehension of the fact that if there is to be salvation at all, it is God alone who wills and accomplishes it. By faith alone is a necessary statement because only in this way can we bring out the essential truth: by grace alone, which means ultimately only: by Christ alone. As Cranmer himself sums it up at the conclusion of the first part, "our justification doth come freely by the mere mercy of God, and of so great and free mercy, that whereas all the world was not able of themselves to pay any part towards their ransom, it pleased our heavenly Father, of his infinite mercy, without any our desert or deserving, to prepare for us the most precious jewels of Christ's body and blood, whereby our ransom might be fully paid, the law fulfilled, and his justice fully satisfied. So that Christ is now the righteousness of all them that truly do believe in him. He for them paid their ransom by his death: he for them fulfilled the law in his life: so that now in him, and by him, every true christian man may be called a fulfiller of the law; forasmuch as that which their infirmity lacketh, Christ's justice hath supplied".[17]

This being the case, Cranmer was at pains to make it clear that faith is not in any way a work of justification, and in that sense a self-justifying work.[18] If in justification there is a twofold office, that of God to man and that of man to God,[19] the two are not coincident. For justification itself is "the office

---

15. P.S., II, p. 128.
16. P.S., II, p. 129.
17. P.S., II, p. 130.
18. P.S., II, p. 132.
19. P.S., II, p. 131.

of God only".[20] It is not something which we can give, but something which we can only receive and take "by his free mercy, and by the only merit of his most dearly beloved Son, our only Redeemer, Saviour, and Justifier, Jesus Christ".[21] It cannot be said, therefore, that "this our own act to believe in Christ, or this our faith in Christ, which is within us, doth justify us, and merit our justification to us (for that were to count ourselves to be justified by some act or virtue that is within ourselves)".[22] Faith is no more to be regarded as a work or virtue than "hope, charity, repentance, dread, and fear of God within us".[23] It has to be renounced as a work in exactly the same way as every other work. When we trust in Christ, we do not rest in ourselves. Faith says as it were: "It is not I that take away your sins, but it is Christ only".[24] In this sense faith is always a passive thing in justification. Its function is not to act or do, but simply to take. It is important, not because it is a primary or supreme work of man, but because it is the appointed and indeed the exclusive means to receive the work of God.

Cranmer repeats this point, for his defence of the word "only" obviously hinges upon it. The Bible itself does not use the word in this context. It can therefore be attacked by the traditionalists as an exaggeration or even a distortion of the Pauline doctrine. We are saved by faith, but we are also saved by hope, or charity, or repentance, or all these things. In reply, Cranmer has of course some quotations from "the old, ancient fathers of the church" to prove that there is nothing novel about the word.[25] But his main contention is that the "only" is simply an equivalent of "without works".[26]

The point of the "only" is not to single out faith as a pre-eminent work or even a special work, but to exclude all works. Indeed, Cranmer will go so far as to exclude faith itself if it is regarded as a work or merit: "And because all this is brought to pass through the only merits and deservings of our Saviour Christ, and not through our merits, or through the merits of

---

20. P.S., II, p. 131.
21. P.S., II, p. 131.
22. P.S., II, pp. 131-132.
23. P.S., II, p. 132.
24. P.S., II, p. 132.
25. P.S., II, pp. 130-131, 131-133.
26. P.S., II, pp. 131, 133.

any virtue that we have within us, or of any work that cometh from us, therefore, in that respect of merit and deserving, we renounce, as it were, altogether again faith, works, and all other virtues."[27] If attention is focused on faith only, it is because in faith it is not focused on ourselves or our works, but only on Jesus Christ.

The new emphasis on faith necessitated a reconsideration of the nature and character of faith, for obviously the justifying faith of Paul and the reformers is rather more than the intellectual assent or infused habit which passed for faith in a good deal of contemporary discussion. In this question as in justification generally Cranmer followed the general lines of Luther's understanding. There are two kinds of faith.[28] The one is a dead belief, which accepts the facts and doctrines of the Christian faith, but does not have an inward trust in Christ, or live out the Gospel in daily obedience.[29] The other includes an acceptance of the facts and doctrines of Christianity, but it also involves "a sure trust and confidence in God's merciful promises",[30] which necessarily expresses itself in life and conduct. It is only this latter faith, the true, lively, and Christian faith of the second homily, which avails for justification.

The element of personal conviction is strongly underlined by Cranmer. Faith is confidence and therefore an inward relationship. But Cranmer does not insist on this aspect in such a way as to make faith only an emotional and pietistic experience. The difference between justifying and non-justifying faith is not that the one is intellectual and the other emotional, for a true faith includes intellectual and volitional as well as more narrowly emotional elements. The difference rather is that the former is outward and dead, the latter inward and alive. The former is idle, barren, and unfruitful, the latter goes to the very root of our being and is therefore quick or lively.[31] Faith, of course, is passive in relation to the work of God. It is only the hand which takes, or the vessel which can be filled. But this does not mean that faith is a weak or bloodless thing. On the contrary, "it liveth and stirreth inwardly

---

27. P.S., II, p. 133.
28. P.S., II, p. 135.
29. *Loc. cit.*
30. *Loc. cit.*
31. *Loc. cit.*

in the heart",[32] and this means that it is robust and active. For although faith cannot plead any good works before God, not even faith itself as a work, all the same "it is lively and fruitful in bringing forth good works".[33] Faith is passive in the sense that it cannot create but can only receive the justifying righteousness which is the gift of God Himself. But faith is active in the sense that receiving righteousness it necessarily impels to those works which are not merely the accompaniment but the expression and outworking of justification.

Cranmer seems to have been particularly sensitive to the possible charge or danger of antinomianism. The whole point of the second and third homilies is to meet this misunderstanding. He was, of course, thinking in terms of definite edification, for, incredible as it may seem to-day, the *Homilies* were meant for general use in the pulpit. He saw clearly that at all costs there must be avoided the dissemination of a comfortable notion that we have only to believe the creed and we can do as we like. The traditionalists were making the most of the dangerous pastoral and ethical implications, and on the current understanding of faith the peril was not by any means illusory. Even for those who understand the doctrine there is a genuine temptation to separate between faith and obedience, absolutizing the formal or functional distinction which evangelical truth does of course demand. But for those who do not understand and perhaps do not want to understand the "by faith only", the inefficacy of works is an obvious and facile excuse for their absence. It is, therefore, quite understandable that Cranmer goes to very great pains to state and to illustrate the relationship between a true faith and the works which God has before ordained that we should walk in them.

There are two main points upon which Cranmer strongly insists, and they are both positive. The first is that where there is a true faith there is a necessary compulsion to good works.[34] It is not just that faith applauds or advises or even encourages works. Works are the necessary consequence. This is the truth for which James contends, although strangely

---

32. P.S., II, p. 136.
33. *Loc. cit.*
34. P.S., II, p. 136.

enough Cranmer does not refer to him in this context.[35] He finds his scriptural evidence in John I,[36] and more especially in the examples of Hebrews II: "This (i.e., faith) made Noe to build the ark. This made Abraham to forsake his country", and so on.[37] Of course, these instances are all taken from the Old Testament, but this does not affect the argument, for Cranmer can quote both Paul and Augustine to show that "the time is altered, but not the faith".[38] "The lively knowledge and faith of God bringeth forth good works."[39] Good works are therefore a test by which a true faith can be discerned from a false. "The trial of all these things is a very godly and christian life."[40]

That is the one side. But there is another side as well. For, as Cranmer puts it, "without faith can no good work be done acceptable and pleasant unto God".[41] If faith is so tied to works that without works there is obviously no faith, the converse is also true, that works are so tied to faith that without faith there are no works. It is a fact, of course, that unbelievers can say and do and think things which are apparently right. But "without faith they are only dead representations without life or any manner of moving. They do appear to be lively works, and indeed they be but dead, not availing to the eternal life."[42] Unfortunately, Cranmer does not elaborate this distinction, nor does he introduce the Lutheran notion of a purely human or civil righteousness. He apparently means that those who do not have faith can go through the outward motions of goodness but they do not have the inward life which is faith itself. They may do things which are in a sense good, but they are not themselves good and therefore the acts are not genuinely good by a deeper and more searching judgment. However, Cranmer does not develop the argument, but clinches his point by some quotations from the Bible and some trenchant passages from Augustine, Ambrose and Chrysostom.[43] The rest of the discussion is devoted to a characterization of good works

---

35. Although cf. P.S., II, p. 137.
36. P.S., II, pp. 138-139.
37. P.S., II, pp. 137-138.
38. P.S., II, p. 138.
39. *Loc. cit.*
40. P.S., II, p. 139.
41. P.S., II, p. 141.
42. *Loc. cit.*
43. P.S., II, pp. 141-143.

in which he singles out the weightier matters of the law from the externalities of religious practice which constantly threaten to engulf or replace them.[44]

It can hardly be pretended that in this matter of justification Cranmer has anything very new to say. All his main points can be paralleled in Luther and Zwingli before him as well as Calvin and other contemporary writers. But what he does say he says clearly and forcibly, showing a fine grasp of the essentials of the Reformation position and an ability to express them not merely with clarity but with theological warmth and a fine pastoral responsibility. The qualities in Cranmer's presentation are perhaps the qualities which are most needed to-day, for writing to some extent defensively he safeguards the doctrine against the chief misconceptions both of his own and subsequent generations.

A first strength in Cranmer's statement is his linking of justification by faith with patristic as well as Pauline sources. A common charge against the doctrine is that it rests on a peculiar and rather strained interpretation of individual texts in Paul. This interpretation was not known until the time of Luther, and ultimately it did not derive from the Bible but from the personal religious experience of Luther himself. Cranmer, however, destroyed this objection by quoting quite a number of passages from the fathers which support justification by faith alone, refusal to distinguish in this matter between ethical and ceremonial works, and a derivation of true works only from faith. No doubt other passages can be quoted from the fathers which point in a rather different direction. That is one of the disadvantages (or should we say the advantages?) of the patristic appeal. But this much at least may be said. The doctrine of justification by faith is not a novel doctrine of which there is no trace at all in the primitive church.

In relation to the substance of the teaching, the second main strength of Cranmer is his strict objectivization of the doctrine by an emphasis on the grace of God and His reconciling action in Jesus Christ. Here, perhaps, more than at any other point, the doctrine has been grossly misunderstood and misrepresented,

---

44. P.S., II, pp. 143 f.

especially in the period of exaggerated subjectivism which is one of the legacies of German Romanticism. There is no doubt, of course, that many Protestants of the new age have compromised the doctrine by a restatement in subjectivist terms. But in point of fact nothing could be further from the mind of Cranmer, or indeed of any of the reformers, than to emphasize the believing subject, or in any way to suspend salvation merely on the individual decision or the emotional reaction of faith. In the matter of salvation, as we have seen, faith is passive or negative. It is simply the hand which receives. Now in its own way receiving is important. Indeed, we can say that it is vital. Without receiving there is no gift for me. But all the same, receiving is subsidiary or secondary to the gift itself, without which there cannot be even the possibility of receiving. In this case the gift is the divine forgiveness and renewal in Jesus Christ, and without this not even faith itself can justify. The primary thing is not the subjective state of faith itself, but the object of faith which in this instance is also its true subject, that is to say, Jesus Christ Himself. If Cranmer had a complaint against the traditionalist. teaching it is not that it was not sufficiently subjective but that it was far too subjective. Theoretically, of course, it still gave the glory to God, but in practice it concentrated attention on the meritorious acts of man. It had lost the Christocentricity which is the only guarantee of true objectivity. Ultimately, perhaps, the failure was in relation to the atoning action of Christ as a genuinely representative, or as Cranmer might have said, substitutionary action. With a true insight, Cranmer began his statement with a short exposition of the atonement. His concern throughout was not to glorify faith and its subjectivity, but to glorify the objective and redemptive reality of Jesus Christ Himself in His person and work.

Yet while that is all true, we have to add at once that Cranmer's presentation has this further strength, that it does mean a subjectivization in the sense of a personalizing of Christianity, and that it avoids therefore the extemalism which always menaces an objective doctrine. The personalization is on two sides. On the one hand, the gift of God as Cranmer understands it is not a nebulous or quantitative grace, but Jesus Christ Himself with all His benefits. On the other hand, faith is not an impersonal acceptance of facts or dogmas, but that confidence in a person, that confiding of oneself to a person which is a concern of the whole man. At bottom, it is the Person who is trusted that is important, not the person who trusts. But on both sides the relationship is at the deepest possible level of personality, the trust and therefore the love and obedience of the believer responding and corresponding to the grace of the One believed. Of course, even when the doctrine has been misunderstood, this has always been true of the practice of Christianity. Even those who do not see the truth of justification can have a personal trust in Jesus Christ. The merit of the reformers is that they have given a more correct and living statement of what is in fact the relationship between God and man as established by God Himself in Jesus Christ.

There is also the incidental strength of this personalized objectivism that it rebuts at once the possible objection of a righteousness which is merely fictional. Justification by faith does not mean at all that we are righteous because God says so although all the time we know very well that we are not. For one thing, the statement that we are righteous is not a bald pronouncement, but an enacted Word in Jesus Christ. This means that objectively we are righteous because the representative man Jesus Christ has fulfilled the law of righteousness for us, taking away the old life of sin in His death upon the cross, and giving us the new life of righteousness in the power of His resurrection. But again, faith is more than an acceptance of this Word of God which is itself an act of divine power. It is the committal to Jesus Christ which is our identification with Him in His dying and rising again for us. Therefore subjectively we are righteous because we are crucified with Christ, and the life which we now live, we live "by the faith of the Son of God who loved us and gave himself for us". When the justifying sentence is the Word of God which is Jesus Christ, and the faith in which we receive it is a personal relationship to Him, nothing could be more irrelevant than to imagine some kind of judicial sharp practice.

The final strength of Cranmer's statement is that it gives a theological and therefore a true rootage to Christian ethics. In this respect it is thoroughly in line with the Bible, as we can see at once from the New Testament epistles. But in Christian history there has always been a tendency for ethics to break loose from theology and to establish what we might almost call an autonomous kingdom, or at least an *imperium in imperio*. Something of this kind had happened in the Middle Ages. The doctrines of the faith remained. But they had no apparent relevance to religious and ethical practice, except, of course, for the trained theologian who could trace the complicated connections. Indeed, to a certain extent the practical and prudential considerations of ethics could even determine doctrinal questions and development. In the last resort, the aberration was from first to last theological, but ethics divorced from the doctrines of grace contributed to the dogmatic misunderstanding. The result was a theology of religious and ethical self-righteousness in which virtues were advanced as at least a partial ground of justification before God.

Cranmer cut right across this system with his insistence that good works proceed from faith, and therefore from grace, and not *vice versa*. His argument is the good one that what matters primarily is what a man is rather than what he does. Actions may often have an external appearance which is not in the least an indication of their true character. An automaton can perform some of the functions of a man, but that does not make it a man. A non-Christian can perform some of the characteristically Christian acts, but that does not make him a Christian. What matters ultimately is life, which in this case means the new life in Jesus Christ. There can be no genuinely Christian conduct except where there is the Christian life, but where there is this life, out of the new heart of the believer there will necessarily proceed the new words and acts of righteousness. The ethical question can be considered only in this wider theological context.

But the life of the Christian which is a new life in Jesus Christ is the life which begins with the personal identification of faith. This is what determines the high function of faith in relation to Christian works. It does so passively in the sense that looking to Jesus Christ in faith we see what we actually are in the sight of God and we are therefore summoned to be what we are. Faith tells us that the life of sin is over, crucified and judged on the cross, and that the new life of righteousness has begun, created with the raising again of Jesus Christ from the dead. Therefore we have to put off the old man with all his unrighteousness, and to put on the new. We have to set our affection on things above, not on things on the earth. But again, it does so actively because the trust which unites us to Jesus Christ, itself a work of the Holy Spirit, cannot fail to involve both grateful love and obedient discipleship and therefore the active fruits of righteousness and service. As Calvin so finely put it: "It is therefore faith alone which justifies, and yet the faith which justifies is not alone."[45] The doctrine of justification by faith does not open the door to antinomianism. It closes it with a sharp finality. "If these fruits do not follow, we do but mock with God, deceive ourselves, and also other men. Well may we bear the name of christian men, but we do lack the true faith that doth belong thereunto."[46] The door which is opened by this doctrine is the only possible door to a life of positive discipleship. For discipleship is not a self-centred self-justification. It is not a proud and pharisaical attaining. It is the humble following of Jesus Christ the Mediator in the new life which is given in the grace of Christ's atoning death and resurrection and received in the faith which is a committal of self-identification with Christ.

Cranmer does not himself develop all the insights which we can find in his work. Nor does he consider in detail the objections which can be or have been raised. In the *Notes* his object was simply to gather together the texts which supported his view. In the *Homilies* he aimed to give a helpful and constructive statement for the more general instruction of the people. Many of the points are put rather baldly, and in certain respects the whole form of the presentation has dated. On the other hand, Cranmer had a clear and sympathetic appreciation of the biblical insights which characterize the

---

45. Calvin, Tracts III, p. 152.   46. P.S., II, p. 140.

Reformation doctrine of justification, and which reach out further perhaps than even the reformers themselves altogether realized. If he did not make any original or outstanding contribution, it was no small thing to give so plain and satisfying and yet also so warm and inspiring a presentation on so scholarly a basis. For his more extended commentary on the concise utterances of the confession, the English church in particular will always be in Cranmer's debt.

4
The Church and Ministry

Already in the doctrine of Scripture we have touched on certain aspects of Cranmer's doctrine of the church. Yet apart from the discussion of authority, he never made any very detailed investigation of this question. His main interest was claimed by the problem of papal headship, which, if it is still very much alive to-day, does not have for us quite the same urgency or relevance as it had for the reformers. What Cranmer wrote on this matter we can leave on one side, not because it is unimportant, but because it has been generally assimilated in the Protestant churches. We can also leave what he had to say about the organizational aspects of the church, although as Cranmer saw them these always seemed to have a certain doctrinal significance. When these matters are extracted, not a great deal is left. Indeed, it is only incidentally, in a scattered sentence or two, and especially in his answer to Smith's *Preface*, that he develops his own understanding of the church and its nature.

The basis of Cranmer's view is a distinction to which he was almost necessarily driven by the harsh actuality of his age. This is the distinction between what he calls "the holy, elected people of God"[1] as the true church, and the external organization of Rome which wrongly "accounted itself to be the holy, catholic church".[2] This distinction was not altogether new even in the sixteenth century, for apart from the pre-Reformation reformers it is inherent in Augustinian and scholastic teaching and derives ultimately from the parables of the drag-net and the wheat and the tares. But it was certainly given a new sharpness at the time of the Reformation, when not merely individuals, but a whole organization could be indicted for disloyalty to the Bible and therefore to catholic truth. Cranmer himself felt the full poignancy of the situation when

---

1. P.S., I, p. 376.   2. *Loc. cit.*

he had to appeal from what ought to have been the catholic church to a small and scattered company which alone maintained a faithfulness to apostolic truth.

The question arises whether there is not at this point a sectarian impulse in Cranmer as indeed in all the reformers. To ask this question is not necessarily to blame Cranmer. In his own sphere he had the very definite aim of preserving the unity of his church even in the work of reform. That is perhaps the fundamental reason for his caution. He did not want the Reformation to be identified only with a faction. He did not want to cause irreparable division in the church. By a twofold strategy of instruction and slow but steady movement he aimed to carry the church with him in a unity of confession and practice. As against that, however, he found it quite impossible to continue in even a pretence of unity with the see of Rome. Faced with its errors, impieties and "detestable enormities", he could not, even in faith, say of the external organization of Christendom: This is the one, holy, catholic and apostolic church. It was not holy, it was not catholic and it was not apostolic. It could not, therefore, be identified with the church, and to maintain a façade of unity was not only impossible but unnecessary and even wrong. For after all, even if the church is united and sanctified in faith, a genuine faith will show some at least of the fruits of truth and righteousness. But in the Roman communion of his time and country Cranmer did not see these fruits. He saw only a coldness and blindness to biblical and evangelical teaching. He saw only pride, ambition, duplicity and an implacable and ruthless hostility. In the circumstances, we need not be surprised that he drew an obvious parallel with similar situations in the Old and New Testaments, when a distinction had to be drawn between the carnal and the spiritual Israel, and the company of the faithful constituted only a "little flock" discountenanced and persecuted by the external organization of the church. The translator and editor of the *Confutation* was following up a genuine thought of Cranmer himself when he compared the Roman hierarchy with the high priests, the scribes and the Pharisees, "who bare the image and name of the known church at that time, but the truth was with Christ and his little flock".[3]

However that may be, it is interesting that Cranmer does not find easy shelter in the concept of a church which is purely invisible. Of course, he agrees with all the reformers, and no doubt with all Christians, that in the last resort the "holy, elected people of God" are invisible in the sense that the hearts of men are known only to God, and He alone can say who are true believers as compared with deceiving and it may be self-deceived confessors. This is the necessary safeguard against a pure sectarianism, which attempts to forestall the last judgment and gather the true believers into a little group of their own marked off from the generality of professors. It is also a necessary safeguard against the exclusivism which would not only condemn or withdraw from Rome as an apostate church, but consign all its adherents to unbelief and therefore to perdition. If the churches are companies of believers among whom the pure Word of God is preached and the sacraments are duly administered, it is still not impossible that even in apostate Rome there may be those who are taught by the Spirit and therefore have all the truth necessary to salvation. But while this is all true, it is also true that in the sphere of the church as in all other spheres the faith of believers must express itself in concrete life and activity. Therefore as opportunity allows, for example in the Reformation countries, the holy elected people of God will find concretion as a fellowship of the word and sacraments, led and governed with his holy spirit, taught all truth necessary to salvation, gathering together in the name of Christ, and enjoying his rule and presence.[4]

Of the church in the deeper sense as the elect people of God, Cranmer accepts a certain inerrancy and invincibility. "This true faith God preserveth in his holy church still, and will do unto the world's end, maugre the wicked antichrist, and all the gates of hell."[5] Or again: "Truth it is indeed that the church doth never wholly err; for ever in most darkness God shineth unto his elect, and in the midst of iniquity he governeth

---

3. P.S., II, pp. II f.   4. P.S., I, p. 376.   5. *Loc. cit.*

them so with his holy word and Spirit, that the gates of hell prevail not against them."⁶ The inherent difficulty in this concept of infallibility is that the church as a human factor has obviously erred many times and been defeated, so that we cannot say of any particular company of Christians that they cannot and do not err. Indeed, as Cranmer himself points out, the history of the church from creation to the crucifixion is a history of continual apostasy, so that it is no wonder if "the open church is now of late years fallen into many errors and corruptions, and the holy church of Christ is secret and unknown".⁷ We can assert the essential inerrancy and invincibility of the church, but we cannot make the obvious deduction which Smith tried to make: This is the church of Christ, therefore that which it teaches is authoritative and will prevail. We cannot even say: This is what the majority in the church teaches, therefore it is the voice of God. Nor, of course, can we always say, as Barth has recently reminded us: This is the minority view, and therefore it will certainly, be the truth.⁸ The most that we can say is this. In certain times and places the truth will be widely held and taught and proclaimed. In other times and places it will be held and taught and proclaimed only by small groups or even by individuals. But whatever happens, the truth will not wholly perish from the church, for always, as in the dark day of Elijah, "God hath preserved a good number, secret to himself, in his true religion".⁹ In this respect, as in so many others, Cranmer seems to be forced back necessarily upon a concept of invisibility, but the truth is, perhaps, that he is making a declaration of faith. He does not invoke a secret church merely as a facile evasion of the difficulty, for his own overmastering concern is that the visible church should itself preach the pure Word of God and rightly administer the sacraments.

For a knowledge of the true church, or of the truth within the church, the only test is faithfulness to the Word of God as attested by the Holy Spirit. It is here that the Scripture-principle of Cranmer links up with his doctrine of the church.

---

6. P.S., I, p. 377.
7. P.S., I, pp. 377-378.
8. *Dogmatik*, IV, 1, p. 792.
9. P.S., I, p. 378.

The church can be defined and accepted as such only in relation to the Bible. Even from the point of view of external organization, one of the primary functions of the church is to be. "as it were a register or treasury to keep the books of God's holy will and testament, and to rest only thereupon".[10] But from a more inward standpoint, the true church will be that company of professing Christians, or those individual Christians, who in doctrine and practice are always reformed and reformable by the Word of God. It is the church "that concerning the faith containeth itself within God's word, not that deviseth daily new articles contrary to God's word: the church, that by the true interpretation of scripture and good example gathereth people unto Christ, not that by wrasting of the scripture and evil example of corrupt living draweth them away from Christ".[11]

This, then, is the doctrine of the church which emerges incidentally from Cranmer's writings. There is no systematic discussion, but on the other hand there is no doubt that these are the basic elements in Cranmer's thinking on the problem. The doctrine has all the strength and the weaknesses of that of the Reformation generally. As everywhere, it is coloured and to some extent moulded by a situation in which the acknowledged church had obviously departed from the scriptural and catholic norm, and those who contended for evangelical and primitive truth were in a relative minority. The empirical relevance of the doctrine gives to it an urgency and realism which mark it off from any idealistic or doctrinaire theorizing. Cranmer had real problems to grapple with and they were complicated and baffling problems. In many respects his solution is a rough and ready one, which he himself has obviously not thought through, but which does at least correspond in some sort to the actuality of the case. If it is not entirely satisfying, it is always realistic. Indeed, we can go further and say that in two respects, or possibly three, he has seized on basic and essential truths without which there can never be a true understanding of the church.

---

10. P.S., I, p. 377.
11. P.S., I, p. 378.

First, it can hardly be denied that the Word and the Spirit are the true and only norm not only of the church's teaching but also of its very life. The norm is objective in so far as we have it in the word written. As we have seen already in relation to Scripture, without this norm there can be no check on the church's development. Claiming always the internal illumination of the Spirit, it can change itself in so radical a way that it becomes something quite other than what it was and what it is meant to be. But the norm is also subjective in the Holy Spirit interpreting and applying Scripture. Without the Spirit the church will necessarily become a moribund institution, strangled by legal regulations and propositions. Cranmer has not developed the thought, but in the conjunction of Word and Spirit he has given us the genuine point of reference for the truth and life of the church.

But second, in his unmistakable bias to the hiddenness or invisibility of the church, Cranmer is obviously feeling after the truth that in its basic qualities of oneness and holiness and catholicity and apostolicity the church has to be believed. In this as in every matter of salvation we do not walk by sight but by faith. He realized, of course, that it is the task of the church to attain these qualities in its concrete life in the world. He did not make the mistake of what we might call a pietistic antinomianism: that the true church will always exist spiritually and therefore it does not too greatly matter what happens to the external church historically. But he also avoided the tempting aberration of the separatist, that by a process of rigid exclusivism the true church can be attained as a tiny sect, or a tiny aggregation of sects, in the world. In this respect the church is like the individual believer. As the body of Christ, it has a hidden life with God which is also its true life. And in this life, because it is Christ's life, because it is in fact Christ Himself, the church is always one and holy and catholic and apostolic. We do not see this, just as we do not see who are the particular members. In the concretions of history the church will often deny its true character just as the Christian will deny his true righteousness. It has to become, or to be what it is. But in faith we accept it for what it is. The strange thing is that Cranmer is not taught by his doctrine of justification to put it quite in this way. But there is no doubt that this is the insight to which he is at least feeling his way with his dialectic of the true church and the false.

That leads us to the final point, that Cranmer has a vivid awareness of the tension which must always characterize the life of the church in the world. Whether he has described it rightly or not is a matter for question. His emphasis is all upon the hiddenness and littleness of the church. These are, of course, biblical concepts, for the real life of Christians is hid with Christ in God, and although many are called, we are told by Christ Himself that few are chosen. All the same, with Cranmer as with most of the reformers we have a suspicion that at this point their doctrine is determined by actualities rather than by the Word of God. We must also ask whether he has penetrated to the real depth of the tension, which is of course inherent in the whole Christian situation, not merely by virtue of the incarnation of Jesus Christ (to which it is in many respects analogous), but by virtue of His atoning death and resurrection. The church has a new life which is the divine-human life of Christ incarnate, crucified and resurrected. But it has this treasure in an earthen vessel. It has to live out this new life in the concrete environment and conditions of the old. That is the real tension of the church. That is the explanation of its continual apostasy and self-contradiction.

But we must not be too hard on Cranmer. If there is an *ad hoc* quality about his statements which indicates that he had hardly seen through to the heart of the matter, he never attempts a thorough or systematic discussion of the question. His course is hazardous and perhaps opportunist, but in avoiding the great and ugly cliff of institutionalism he does not make shipwreck on the successive reefs of sectarianism and ecclesiastical antinomianism. If his analysis of the tension in the church is inadequate, he does at least reckon with the actuality of the tension, and he shows an awareness at least of its basic and essential character.

Closely bound up with the church are of course the "orders of ministers who by a common speaking among the people are called the church, or men of the church".[12] Cranmer himself did not approve this popular identification, nor did he accept either the validity or necessity of the various sub-orders. However, these are points which he did not actually discuss: they have to be inferred from his actions and writings. On the other hand, there are clear references in different places,[13] especially if we include the preface to the Ordinal[14] and the article (36), to show that Cranmer regarded the threefold ministry as of apostolic derivation and therefore to be continued in the church. From a very early date, too, he both preached and practised clerical marriage. As he saw it, this was a disciplinary question in which the church's legislative authority was plainly restricted by New Testament precept and precedent. Rather oddly, we do not have any written argument in defence of this position, but there is no doubt that from the time of the divorce question he found here another example of the illegitimate interference of the church with the indisputable law of the Bible. It is unfortunate that his opposition to the Six Articles on this point has not survived, as in addition to his public speeches he seems to have made a strenuous effort to convert Henry to his view. At his examination he appealed to the civil law, but this was only in respect of the open and public acknowledgment of his marriage, not of its essential rightness.[15] Perhaps the best surviving evidence of his thinking on the matter is in the short summary of the article (32).

These questions were not of primary doctrinal importance, but the same cannot be said of the clear rejection of orders as a true sacrament of the Gospel. In spite of the teaching of the *King's Book*, for which he himself was not responsible, Cranmer had evidently been rethinking this whole issue of sacramental definition even prior to 1540. He allowed with all the reformers that there is in Scripture a loose usage of the basic term *mysteria* to include marriage or the incarnation or even the *mysterium iniquitatis*.[16] Taking the term in this wider sense, the number

---

12. P.S., II, p. 515.
13. Cf. P.S., II, p. 116.
14. P.S., II, p. 519.
15. P.S., II, p. 220.
16. P.S., II, p. 115.

of the sacraments could not be restricted to two or even to seven, for "all the figures which signify Christ to come, or testify that he is come, be called sacraments".[17] For this reason the fathers themselves never deliberately selected the usual seven, so that *prima facie* there is no reason whatever either in Scripture or the fathers to adopt the traditional classification.[18] On the other hand, if we take the word in its deeper or stricter sense, and consider "the matter, nature and effect" of the sacraments, Cranmer argues that a case can be made out for penance and marriage as well as baptism and eucharistia, but "of the matter, nature and effect of the other three, that is to say, confirmation, orders, and extreme unction, I read nothing in the scripture, as they be taken for sacraments".[19] At a later date he would extend his doubts to penance and marriage as well, for in the thirties he was only feeling his way on this matter of the sacraments. But he was quite clear and definite on the matter of ordination, denying that there is any more promise of grace "in the committing of the ecclesiastical office, than in the committing of the civil office".[20]

With the discussion of this point there is linked a survey of the whole question of clerical ordination and appointment.[21] It is extremely brief, but it is also extremely radical. The striking feature of it is the extent of Lutheran influence and the corresponding Erastian impulse. Cranmer assumes quite calmly that in a Christian commonwealth the appointment, assignation and election of ecclesiastical no less than civil officers belongs properly to the Crown.[22] If a different order obtained in the New Testament and primitive days, when ministers were either commended by the apostles or elected by the people, this was due only to the lack of a civil head. "The divers comely ceremonies and solemnities used in the admission of these offices are not of necessity, but only for a good order and seemly fashion."[23] If Cranmer means by this, as he seems to mean, that even ordination itself is a dispensable or alterable ceremony, he has gone to the furthest possible extreme from

---

17. P.S., II, p. 115.
18. *Loc. cit.*
19. P.S., II, p. 116.
20. *Loc. cit.*
21. P.S., II, pp. 116-117.
22. P.S., II, p.116.
23. *Loc. cit.*

the medieval sacramentalism of orders, and much further than most of his Anglican successors would be prepared to go. For while it is the classical Anglican position that the form of the ministry and its appointment and the ceremonial of admission are all indifferent and therefore variable, it is accepted that there is something essential about order itself, and that ministerial ordination is normally to be retained. But of course Cranmer had no wish to deny this. He was simply arguing that while there has to be a ministry, and ministers must be publicly called, the mode of calling is not fixed by Scripture, but belongs to the sphere of things in which the church can take order for itself. The same is true of the actual form of the ministry. Cranmer himself favoured a retention of the threefold form which as he saw it had obviously come down from primitive and apostolic days. But the succession as Cranmer saw it has historical and pragmatic rather than doctrinal significance. Neither the validity nor, if the church itself so determines, the regularity of the ministry is affected in the least by the absence of historical linkage. The preservation of the threefold order is plainly regarded as desirable, but it is not of absolute necessity.

Indeed, on examination the threefold order cannot be sustained as scriptural, for Cranmer cannot find any real distinction between the episcopate and the presbyterate either in origin or character: "The bishops and priests were at one time, and were not two things, but both one office in the beginning of Christ's religion."[24] In other words, if we make this a matter of doctrine and not of order, we shall have to abandon the time-honoured distinction of three main offices in the church. But Cranmer himself cannot agree that the actual form of the ministry is more than a matter of organization, or the external mode of appointment and admission more than a matter of ceremonial.

For this reason he insists that at a pinch the ceremony of consecration is unnecessary, and that in special circumstances the ministry can be reconstituted, or even constituted for the first time, either by civil enactment or on the initiative of the civil power. For instance, "if it befortuned a

---

24. P.S., II, p. 117.

prince christian-learned to conquer certain dominions of infidels, having none but temporal-learned men with him", it is lawful and indeed obligatory that "he and they should preach and teach the word of God there, and also make and constitute priests".[25] Or again, if for some reason the ordinary succession of ministers failed, as happened in some of the reforming territories, Cranmer thought it both right and necessary that the Christian laity responsible for ordinary government should re-establish the ministry. It is against this background that we have to consider not only his proposal to derive ecclesiastical offices from the Crown, but his authorization of the ordinal by Parliament as well as Convocation, and the very cautious wording of the article: "by men who have public authority given unto them, in the congregation, to call and send ministers unto the Lord's vineyard" (23).

Erastianism could hardly go further, and it would appear that in Cranmer's thinking the ministry has been almost completely overwhelmed by the royal supremacy. Of course, there is a credit side as well, for Cranmer avoids without question the evil not only of a dogmatic papalism but also of a dogmatized institutionalism. The supposed doctrines of a grace of orders and a necessary episcopal succession are subjected to the rigorous and destructive scrutiny of Scripture. He sees that the ministry must not be enslaved or distorted either by a pseudo-sacramentalism or by the ideologizing of an impressive but not by any means indispensable fact. But as against this, he has an exaggerated view of the civil authority which we can hardly describe as anything other than disastrous. He allows to the Christian prince an immediate and dogmatic sanction which he nowhere seems to ascribe to the Christian minister. He does not deny perhaps, but he certainly does not emphasize, that the ministry too has its own direct authorization as well as the temporal power. Nor does he allow sufficiently that in its external form the civil power is no less subject to the relativities of history than the outward aspect of the ministry. The heart of Cranmer's understanding is not merely that he subjugates the ecclesiastical to the temporal office, but that he

---

25. *Loc. cit.*

seems to oppose to a relativized ministry (which is a matter of order) the absolutized monarchy (which is a matter of divine law).

But we must not exaggerate. Cranmer does not destroy the ministry altogether. Nor does he make it only a department of state. For within the external order there is always the essential element which rests on the divine appointment and commandment. Irrespective of the question of order or organization or ceremonial, the bishop or priest has an evangelical and pastoral function which is not given him by the state, although it may be the duty of a Christian state to see that he exercises it.[26] For a genuine doctrine of the ministry we do not turn to the form of commissioning but to the commission itself. The former is variable, but the latter is unalterably fixed by divine commandment. Or rather, the external form of the commissioning is variable and therefore non-doctrinal. The genuine doctrinal factor is the internal calling and moving of the Holy Spirit which is the indispensable pre-requisite of a true exercise of spiritual functions. It is here in this commission and calling that Cranmer finds the real *esse* of the ministry, and not in the non-essential factors with which traditionalists normally tended to identify it.

The truth is that in relation to the ministry as to the church Cranmer has an awareness of the ineradicable tension or duality. By virtue of its nature, constitution and function, as the ministry of Jesus Christ by the Holy Spirit, it has a divine and therefore an essential, inalienable and dogmatic aspect. It is the ministry of the Gospel. But by virtue of its historical form and character, it has a human and therefore a relative, variable, and pragmatic aspect. The weakness in Cranmer's presentation, as in that of Luther, is that he separates far too sharply between the two aspects, isolating the divine from the human and confining it to an inward and secret sphere which in practice does not and cannot interpenetrate as it should the outward and public. It is true, of course, that as Cranmer sees it neither circumstances nor civil authorities have the right or power to alter the essential ministry. But they do have both

---

26. P.S., II, p. 116.

the right and power to vary the externals of the ministry irrespective of its *esse*, and therefore on occasion to the final detriment of its evangelical proclamation and precept. Yet only in theory, for when it came to the point, in his final arraignment and martyrdom, Cranmer could not allow even the absolute power of the Crown to destroy evangelical truth. He came to this position only after a very serious conflict of loyalties. As he himself pointed out,[27] the conflict is inherent in the very situation, for both the "powers that be" and the ministry are ordained by God, and in a Christian land their responsibilities necessarily overlap. But in Cranmer the conflict was all the more acute because of his very clear-cut distinction between the absolute and relative aspects of the ministry and his subjection of the latter to a very much absolutized monarchy. Neither Calvin on the one hand nor Queen Mary on the other felt the difficulty with quite the same poignancy as Cranmer.

The treatment is fragmentary and in many respects unsatisfactory, yet it has its strong features as well. A first point is this. In principle if not in fact, the insistence on the authority of the prince preserved in Cranmer's teaching the very necessary truth that on its human side the calling and function of the ministry is not narrowly ecclesiastical but ecclesiological: a matter for the whole church. In primary calling the ministry is the ministry of Jesus Christ, and ordination by existing ministers expresses if it does not regulate or canalize this basic aspect. But in secondary calling the ministry is the ministry of the church, and election or appointment by the statutory authority in the congregation expresses again if it does not regulate or canalize this subsidiary aspect. In the, early church when there was no Christian ruler, or indeed at any time when authority is opposed to the faith, the external calling may have to be administered by the people or their accredited representatives. In Tudor England, however, this responsibility devolved naturally upon the monarch, although sometimes in consultation with Convocation and Parliament, and through the recognized machinery of government. For Cranmer, that

---

27. P.S., II, pp. 214-215; 447 f.

seemed, rightly or wrongly, to be the scriptural ideal. But there is another possibility that he does not dispute, but obviously does not envisage for his own country. The "powers that be" are ordained by God, but the form of the "powers" will vary with varying circumstances. In England it may be a Tudor despotism, or it may later become a constitutional monarchy. In Switzerland it may be a city council. In other countries it may become a secularized and neutral or even a hostile government, in which case the external calling will pass back to the congregation and its representatives. The underlying principle, however, is that on its external side the appointment of ministers is not merely a question for a hierarchy but an affair of the whole church, so that no man ought to exercise his ministry without the expressed willingness of the congregation.

The second point we have touched on already, for it is at the heart of the whole discussion. This is the clarity with which Cranmer sees the necessary tension or duality in the ministry. In medieval thinking there had been the tendency to make the essential ministry co-terminous with the given historical factor of bishops, or bishops and presbyters. Cranmer, however, realized that in the ministry as in the church we have to do with a complex. The ministry is not one thing, but two: the one absolute, the other relative; the one doctrinal, the other historical; the one "divine" in Jesus Christ, the other "human" in the world. He himself does not say it, but at bottom this twofoldness reflects the incarnational duality of Christ Himself in the world. It is inescapable for a church which has to live and witness in the world, but which has its true life in Jesus Christ, incarnate, crucified, raised, and ascended for it. The merit of Cranmer is that he brings this tension before us in the starkest possible form, over-emphasizing it no doubt at the expense of the unity, but safeguarding it against a false absorption or confusion.

What is the lesson in all this and its contemporary relevance? We can put it bluntly in this way. The episcopacy itself, the evangelical and pastoral function instituted by Jesus Christ and exercised under the compulsion of the Holy Spirit, is always an absolute. But the episcopate, even in the sense or form of the historical threefold ministry, is only a relative. Or again, succession in the dominical commission is an absolute, but succession in the human form of commissioning is a relative. The absolute and the relative belong together in the one ministry. But only mischief can result when the relative is absolutized, when the essential ministry is identified with this or that contingent form, when what is a legitimate and probably an expedient arrangement is regarded as final and sacrosanct and therefore a norm of the regularity or even the validity not merely of a ministry but of a whole communion. Certainly, there can be no church without the essential ministry, which means episcopacy: the preaching and teaching of the Gospel and the administration of the sacraments and discipline. Not even the Christian prince can overthrow this divinely appointed order. That is the one side. But the other side is that this episcopacy, or essential ministry, does not necessarily involve the medieval or any other structure, not even the threefold order of bishops, priests and deacons, which in spite of its respectable antiquity cannot claim the clear and authoritative sanction of the New Testament.

Cranmer himself made the distinction in a way which is obviously exaggerated. Perhaps he did not draw the line in quite the right place. He certainly drew it too sharply. But it is a line which has been more frequently blurred in the church than over-emphasized. Without it, we miss the Christian and therefore the christological tension of the ministry, and a right understanding is quite impossible. Our debt to Cranmer is, then, that he drew this line at all.

5

Holy Baptism

Cranmer did not give any specific attention to the doctrine of holy baptism. This is strange in many ways, for he was constantly confronted with the question. Of course, he touched on it many times, but except in the article, and possibly even there, he always did so in the context of other doctrines. This being the case, it is not easy to give a coherent account of his teaching, although it will be found that he does in fact cover a very wide tract of baptismal theology.

Two lesser points arose out of his handling of Holy Scripture, and they can be dismissed briefly. In relation to infant baptism, some traditionalists had argued that "it is not contained in the scriptures; and yet this is to be observed upon pain of damnation of the said children".[1] The conclusion, of course, is that this necessary doctrine or practice is grounded solely upon an apostolic tradition.[2] But Cranmer could not accept this example, which as he saw would "open a gap both to the Donatists and to the Anabaptists".[3] He had shown already that Augustine defended infant baptism by John 3:5,[4] as did also the school-men and the Tridentines.[5] He added to this text a short list of passages or references which favour the baptizing of infants: the law of circumcision; the Abrahamic promise; the express invitation of Christ; and the judgment of Paul.[6] His own view was that "by these, and many other plain words of scripture, it is evident that the baptism of infants is grounded upon the holy scriptures".[7]

The case was otherwise, however, with some of the baptismal ceremonies. Trine immersion went back to a very early date, but it had no written sanction in the New Testament, and

---

1. P.S., II, p. 60.
2. *Loc. cit.*
3. *Loc. cit.*
4. P.S., II, p. 59.
5. Cf. Lombard, IV, *Dist.* 4; *A Catechism of Trent*, II, 2, qu. 31.
6. P.S., II, p. 60.
7. *Loc. cit.*

therefore it could not be classed as necessary.⁸ It resembled the honey and milk of the age of Tertullian, which had not in fact survived in the medieval church.⁹ Whatever significance may be found in these ceremonies, for example, a trinitarian reference in trine immersion, they are matters which a church has power to accept, vary or discontinue "for a decent order and conformity in the church".¹⁰ In 1552 Cranmer's own church exercised this authority to maintain the sign of the cross but to abolish every other ceremony, including trine immersion.

The doctrine of justification also involved a brief consideration of baptism, although unfortunately Cranmer did not develop in detail the relevant problems. The issue was this. A traditionalist like Stephen Gardiner accepted a prior justification in baptism when the soul is cleansed and made righteous by virtue of the sacramental action.¹¹ But then the committing of new sin gave rise to a new problem of justification, and it was in this connection that the sacrament of penance and the virtues of faith, hope and charity became necessary to justification. But Cranmer's re-thinking of justification, and therefore of baptism, necessarily involved a complete reconsideration of the baptismal work and remission. In the absence of a full discussion it is difficult to say with certainty how Cranmer viewed this question. On the one hand, he sometimes uses terms which have at least a suggestion of the traditional interpretation.¹² On the other, it is evident that the baptismal cleansing is very strictly related to the representative work of Jesus Christ, and that it extends, on repentance, to every subsequent sin.¹³ From this it follows that the baptized person is never righteous in himself, by a sacramentally operated activity of the Holy Spirit, but is always reckoned righteous (because in a very true sense he is righteous) in Jesus Christ. It also follows that the former sacrament of penance is subsumed in baptism.¹⁴ Since the baptismal righteousness is in Jesus Christ, it cannot be lost by sin so long as there is a re-entry into Jesus

---

8. P.S., II, p. 58.
9. *Loc. cit.*
10. P.S., II, p. 59.
11. Cf. Foxe, VI, p. 50.

12. Cf. P.S., II, p. 128.
13. *Loc. cit.*
14. *Loc. cit.*, and cf. p. 116.

Christ in penitence and faith. There is also an ethical implication. The Christian life is not a rather hopeless struggle to maintain the given righteousness of baptism, and in that way either to avoid slipping back into perdition or to cut down the necessary purgatorial period. It is a translation into terms of sight, of this life, of the righteousness which is eternally accomplished in Jesus Christ and apprehended and enjoyed in faith. The real baptismal work, indeed the true baptism, is the representative action of Jesus Christ, which is itself the finished work of remission and renewal.

If he had been writing a fuller and more doctrinal treatise on justification Cranmer could hardly have avoided these basic and vital themes. He had to face them again, this time from a different angle, when he gave himself to a fuller study of the eucharistic question. The importance of baptism in relation to holy communion is easily seen, for according to his later teaching these two alone are full sacraments of the Gospel. But if they are both sacraments instituted by Christ and administered in the power of the Spirit, we can be sure that the action of God in the one sacrament will be of the same kind as His action in the other. The divine presence and operation in communion can therefore best be understood by a comparison with the divine presence and operation in baptism. For this reason the statements in the *True and Catholic Doctrine* do contain incidentally a fairly detailed discussion of baptism. The fact that it is incidental does not mean that it is peripheral or unimportant. For it is in these passages that Cranmer is at grips with the main sacramental problem.

A first and a very significant point is that Cranmer accepts a definite presence of Jesus Christ Himself in the administration of baptism. He is replying to the hazardous distinction of Gardiner between a presence of the spirit of Christ in baptism and the presence of His body and blood in the Lord's supper.[15] This, he says, is not only "blasphemous against the ineffable unity" *of* Christ's person,[16] but it is also "no small derogation to baptism, wherein we receive not only the spirit of Christ; but also Christ himself, whole body and soul, manhood and

---

15. P.S., I, p. 22.   16. P.S., I, p. 157.

Godhead, unto everlasting life".[17] He then quotes the apostle Paul to the effect that baptism no less than communion is a putting on of Christ, the one in respect of regeneration, the other of "nourishment and augmentation".[18] This presence is, of course, rightly associated with the coming of the Holy Spirit, and it is in this sense primarily that Cranmer thinks and speaks of it as a spiritual presence. The spiritual presence of Christ is not just a presence of Christ's spirit, nor is it only a presence of Christ in or to our spirit. It is a presence of Christ by the Holy Spirit in accordance with the teaching and promise of the Johannine discourses on the Paraclete: "I will not leave you comfortless"; "I will come to you". The primary relevance of the argument is obviously to the eucharistic presence, but it has a general importance for our understanding of the whole sacramental and evangelical operation. Christ incarnate, crucified, risen and glorified is contemporaneously present in the administration of word and sacrament, not because He Himself is corporally there, but because He is present by the Spirit of promise who is also called the Spirit of Christ.

This presence of Christ in baptism is, of course, an effective presence. Christ comes by the Holy Spirit in order to do a definite work of grace. It is not only the incarnate Christ who comes, but Christ crucified, risen and ascended. By its very nature, therefore, baptism "exhibits"[19] to us, not simply Christ, but especially Christ crucified and risen. It is a declaration of that cross which Christ described both as His cup and also as His baptism. But like the word of the cross it is a declaration or exhibition in and by which Christ is present by the Holy Spirit to incorporate us into Himself crucified and risen for us, to do the work of regeneration which is our entry into His redemptive person and work. In Cranmer's phrase, the baptized are "clothed" or "apparelled with Jesus Christ".[20] He means that they put on Jesus Christ, or that they are inserted into Him, so that they too are crucified and raised with Him. Thus the work of baptism is a work of regeneration leading to

---

17. P.S., I, p. 25.
18. *Loc. cit.*
19. P.S., I, p. 156.
20. P.S., I, p. 71.

sanctification and ultimately to the resurrection from the dead.

Cranmer is most careful not to equate either the presence of Christ or the effective operation of the Spirit directly with the baptismal water. He acknowledges that the water undergoes a sacramental change, which can be marked, of course, by a dedicatory prayer. But the change is not a magical change in the element. It is a change in the use to which it is put. It is a change into "the proper nature and kind of a sacrament",[21] signifying "the wonderful change which Almighty God by His omnipotency worketh really in them that be baptized therewith".[22] It is for this reason that the water is often called *aqua regenerans* or *aqua sanctificans*.[23] "The water doth not regenerate in deed".[24] Nor is the Holy Spirit actually in the water. But being set apart for a sacramental use, it is given the name of the regenerative work of which it is the sacrament. Cranmer put this very clearly in the discussion of a patristic quotation: "And where you allege Emissen for the conversion of the substance of bread and wine, this conversion, as Emissen saith, and as I have declared before, is like our conversion in baptism, where outwardly is no alteration of substance (for no sacramental alteration maketh alteration of the substance), but the marvellous and secret operation is inwardly in our souls."[25]

The marvellous and secret operation does not take place in all those who receive the sacrament. This is a crucial point in Cranmer's baptismal interpretation. It was not altogether a new point, for the school-men and the fathers before them had always insisted that insincerity or unbelief can oppose an obstacle to sacramental grace. In this sense a worthy reception is clearly essential to sacramental efficacy. Cranmer puts it in this way: "Those that come feignedly, and those that come unfeignedly, both be washed with the sacramental water, but both be not washed with the Holy Ghost, and clothed with Christ."[26] The distinction itself is old enough, but in Cranmer's treatment there are some new emphases which take us right to the heart of his baptismal reinterpretation.

---

21. P.S., I, p. 180.
22. *Loc. cit.*
23. P.S., I, p. 150.
24. *Loc. cit.*
25. *Loc. cit.*
26. P.S., I, p. 221.

First, the critical factor in worthy reception is quite obviously faith, which does not mean for Cranmer the acceptance of a creed or even sincerity of acceptance or of the baptismal desire, but the inward confidence and trust in Christ which avails to justification. He does not make it quite plain how this faith is related to the sacramental operation. It is certainly not a habit infused by it. In many cases, e.g., adult converts, faith in Cranmer's sense precedes the sacramental administration, and therefore the grace is present prior to the sign. In other cases, e.g., infants, the faith may not be present until some time later. In all cases, however, Cranmer is insistent that without faith the sacrament cannot be received inwardly and effectively and therefore to spiritual profit. This necessity of faith is the link between his doctrine of justification and his doctrine of baptismal efficacy.

But second, the distinction between external and internal reception means that Cranmer finds in baptism the same incarnational duality as he finds in the church and the ministry. This is perhaps the true answer to that obvious problem of time which we find in the relationship between faith and baptism. Baptism as a sacrament has two aspects. It is not one thing but two things. There is the external washing of water and there is the internal washing of the Spirit. This duality is the whole point of a sacrament, which comprises both a sign and a thing signified. In the full sense of the term baptism means both the sign and the thing signified. It is a baptism with water and it is also a baptism with the Holy Ghost and with fire. But because there is a unity of the two aspects or "natures", this does not mean that there is confusion, as in the rigid identification of grace with the actual element. Without the Spirit, which will mean in effect without faith, only the water can be administered. The sign is present, and therefore every recipient has the sign of regeneration and can be described as sacramentally regenerate.[27] But the presence of the sign does not carry with it the automatic concomitant of the thing signified, at any rate in its subjective reality. Nor is the thing signified so tied to the administration

---

27. P.S., I, *pp. 221 f.*

of the sign that it cannot be present without it. The most that can be said is that where the sign is administered the objective reality of Christ crucified and risen for us is always there, although not always perceived or accepted, and that the Holy Spirit is always seeking through the word and the sign to move to an inward as well as an outward identification in personal crucifixion and renewal.

It is in the light of this distinction that Cranmer explains the baptism of infants, who cannot make any profession of faith, and of whom it can never be affirmed with even a normal degree of human certainty that they actually have faith. Why then do we baptize infants, and allow the sponsors to make for them a Christian confession? On this point Cranmer "rehearsed" the answer of Augustine to Boniface who had asked this same question: "after a certain manner of speech ... the sacrament of faith is faith. And to believe is nothing else but to have faith; and therefore when we answer for young children in their baptism, that they believe, which have not yet the mind to believe, we answer that they have faith, because they have the sacrament of faith. And we say also that they turn unto God, because of the sacrament of conversion unto God; for that answer pertaineth to the celebration of the sacrament."[28] This is the reason why in spite of his refusal to identify the sign and the thing signified Cranmer can still make a categorical assertion of regeneration in the baptismal office. Even children can be described as regenerate, not because we know that in each individual case there has been an inward operation and renewal, not merely because we look forward in the gratitude of faith to a future fulfilment, but because we know that they have the sign and pledge of the grace signified for which we pray and to which we bear witness. In literal fact, of course, our external baptism with water is not our regeneration, but it is called this because it is the sacrament of it, and because baptism in the full sense includes the regeneration which is our entry into the baptism of Christ. The external washing with water is the "humanity" of the sacrament to which the "divinity" is conjoined when there

---

28. P.S., I, p. 124.

is the demonstration of the Spirit and of power, and therefore a baptism in the true and full sense. Objectively, no doubt, it is possible to say that there is always this conjunction, but subjectively – and this is the point and goal of the administration of word and sacrament – it may often enough be the case that there is only an external reception and therefore only a sacramental regeneration: the sign, but not the thing signified.

By its very constitution the baptismal teaching of Cranmer is fragmentary and disconnected. It occurs only in the context of other questions, and no point is ever worked out in detail or for its own sake. There is also a fair amount of repetition, and the various pieces have to be fitted together from many different places. Yet in spite of these very evident deficiencies the doctrine as a whole has a certain clarity and depth which show that Cranmer had given it a considerable amount of thought. Even in its secondary capacity baptism had for Cranmer a position of pre-eminence, affecting not only the interpretation of the sister-sacrament, but touching the very heart of saving truth in the doctrine of justification.

What, then, are the significant points in the fragmentary jottings of Cranmer? The first is his clear relating of Jesus Christ to the Holy Spirit in the understanding of His evangelical and sacramental presence. This very scriptural insight enables Cranmer to avoid the two disruptive extremes which have always threatened the church. On the one hand, we cannot say that Christ is now present with the same immediate and localized presence as in the days of His incarnate life and ministry. To try to have Christ in this way is to do despite to the Holy Spirit, trying to go back behind Pentecost. But on the other hand the action of the Holy Spirit does not mean a "spiritualizing" which destroys altogether any real presence of Christ. To try to have the Spirit in this way is to do despite to Christ Himself, allowing Pentecost to supersede rather than to complement the incarnation and the atonement. As Cranmer so finely sees, the whole point of God's action in word and sacrament is that Christ Himself is now present, but by the Holy Spirit. It is not merely the Logos or the divine Son who is present. It is the Logos incarnate, crucified, resurrected and ascended. To the men of every age and every place He is made a contemporary by the Holy Spirit.

The second point is that Cranmer does at least indicate if he does not develop an inter-connection between baptism and justification. He has not thought out all the implications of this theme, but he has obviously grasped the revolutionary insights of Luther: that the baptismal forgiveness and righteousness are by imputation, not by an actual cleansing, and that the faith required is baptism in not merely credal assent but inward trust and conviction. When the baptismal work is re-examined along these lines, the way opens up for a less formalized and a far more living and dynamic conception in which the evangelical and sacramental aspects will work together rather than against each other.

Third, Cranmer has well seen that in the presentation of Jesus Christ by the Holy Spirit through word and sacrament there is an incarnational tension analogous to that which we find in Jesus Christ Himself. The constant pressure in sacramental theology, as in christology, is to evade or dissolve this duality. The evasion may take the form of a subsuming of the human element into the divine, in which case the result will be a doctrine of automatic efficacy. Or it may take the form of a swallowing up of the divine by the human, in which case nothing will be left but a bare symbolism. Cranmer steers a middle course between the two errors. His primary contention is that the sacrament is two things, and that its unity is an incarnational unity in and by the operation of the Holy Spirit. This insight is plainly essential to any true understanding of baptism.

Yet it can hardly be denied that in Cranmer's own presentation there is what we might call a Nestorian tendency. In his anxiety to avoid an *ex opere operato* view, he does not quite do justice to the real unity of sign and thing signified. Rightly, he suspends this unity on the operation of the Spirit. But as he sees it the operation of the Spirit seems to have almost a capricious quality. From another angle, it is in faith that there is a conjunction of sign and thing signified. This is not meant in a subjectivist sense, for true faith is the work of the Spirit, and to that extent it is itself the inward work of baptism. To have faith is to have regeneration by the Holy Spirit. Therefore, if reception depends on faith, it is because faith is reception. Faith as the work of the sacrament does not derive ultimately from a human choice, but from the sovereign activity of the Spirit. The unity of sign and thing signified is real enough when there is this activity, but with this strictly subjective reference it seems to be an *ad hoc* rather than an essential unity.

The reason for this weakness, and perhaps for the unfinished nature of the relating of justification and baptism, is that Cranmer does not seem to take sufficiently into account the objective reference which is the basic and primary point in his doctrine of justification, the representative action of Jesus Christ in His death and resurrection. In his discussion of sign and thing signified he thinks of regeneration only in terms of the individual application, and his emphasis is therefore upon faith. Now this is necessary. Indeed, in relation to the word and sacraments the personal response is the whole point of the witness and appeal and the goal of the Spirit's work. Neither word nor sacrament has achieved its objective unless there is individual identification with Jesus Christ, which means regeneration from one angle and repentance and faith from another. But that is not the whole story, for the witness of word and sacrament and the basis of their appeal is that death and renewal have already taken place representatively in Jesus Christ. With this objective reference there is always a unity of sign and thing signified, just as there is always a unity of the word and action of man and the word and action of the Spirit. I myself may not believe. I may not be inwardly regenerate. I may not have the true work of baptism. But all the same baptism tells me, not merely that I am sacramentally washed and regenerate, that I have the sign of faith and conversion, but that I am in fact washed and regenerate in the representative Man who has taken my place, so that what has happened to Him has in a very strict sense happened to me and to all men.

Now this is important, for it solves the ultimate dilemma in the relating of justification and baptism as well as the parallel difficulty of the union of sign and thing signified. What Cranmer himself says is true enough. Faith is the point of contact between both baptism and justification and sign and thing signified. But it is only the subjective point of contact. Behind faith there stands the object of faith, the One with whom faith identifies itself because it is in Him and Him alone that God has dealings with man, because He has now taken the place of the sinner and fulfilled for him the movement of death and resurrection. This One, the representative man Jesus Christ, is the primary and objective point of contact between the baptism which attests Him and the justification which He gives, between the sign which is the sign of His cross and the thing signified which is crucifixion and resurrection.

The baptized are the justified. Cranmer himself could say this. But he could say it only in a formal or verbal sense. They are the justified because they have the sacrament of justification. He was right in his rejection of the medieval assertion. The baptized are not the justified because they are made just by a mysterious inward work in virtue of the passion. But he was wrong in his conclusion that there is no real justification at all except where there is faith. From the subjective point of view which he was primarily concerned to emphasize this is true enough. But it is true only because of the deeper truth which he was also concerned to emphasize, that we are objectively justified in Christ crucified and risen for us. We are accounted righteous and we are righteous, not because we have faith, but because God does not have dealings with us at all, but deals instead with the One who has taken our place and in that place died and risen again for us. Not all men enter into Christ or identify themselves with Him. That is where faith comes in. It is the work of the Holy Spirit to bring us to this self-identification. The goal and fulfilment of word and sacrament is this entry into Christ in an analogous movement of penitence and faith. But we can be justified by faith only because we are already justified in Christ whether we accept it and enter into it or not. It is only on the basis of Christ's work done for us, which is the ultimate thing signified of baptism, that there can be the necessary self-identification of penitence and faith which is the subjective work.

Cranmer himself, as we have seen, did not wish to minimize this truth. But there is a danger that in his anxiety to avoid the false objectivism which in effect is always a work in us and therefore subjective, he tended to overlook the primary thing which alone can give sense and unity to the sacrament. The Gospel is not merely that we should have faith, but that we should have faith in Christ: Christ incarnate, crucified and risen. Pneumatology is not enough. Nor is christology. Both the christology and the pneumatology must be soteriological. Between Christmas and Pentecost there must be a place for Good Friday and Easter. This is what we have to allow for in our theology of baptism as in theology generally. It is good to emphasize the necessity of the work of the Spirit. It is good to re-think sacramental operation in accordance with the incarnational pattern. But we shall always be left with insoluble enigmas if we forget that the incarnation is indissolubly linked with the atonement, and that the work of the Spirit is to proclaim and apply the divine action completed in Christ. It is when we think of word and sacrament as the attestation of this action, and therefore, on that basis, as the means of the work of the Spirit, that we can begin to have a genuine insight into their true nature and efficacy.

6

The Eucharistic Presence

As we have seen already, in his sacramental theology the main concern of Cranmer was with the doctrine of Holy Communion. His chief discussion of baptism was in relation to this question. He also devoted to it his only dogmatic treatises of any magnitude. Much of the relevant material is, of course, extremely detailed, especially in the more polemical *Defence* and the rather tiresome and pedantic disputations which have somehow been preserved through Foxe.[1] But through it all there run some interesting and instructive motifs.

Cranmer came to his eucharistic teaching only very slowly, for this was an issue which had divided all the reformers from the very outset. The exact progress of his thinking it is quite impossible to discover. At his examination before Brooks he was charged with holding three contrary doctrines: the traditionalist, the Lutheran and the Zwinglian; but he himself denied this.[2] His own account is that he was never a Lutheran, but that he passed from a traditionalist to a reformed position after consultation "with my Lord of London, doctor Ridley, who by sundry persuasions and authorities of doctors drew me quite from my opinion".[3] There is no doubt that during Henry's reign he had condemned the Zwinglian interpretation as he read it in Vadian[4] and as it was advocated by Lambert. It is also true that in his translation of the catechism of Justus Jonas he deliberately altered the original so as not to propagate the peculiar Lutheran tenet.[5] On the other hand it is possible that Ridley's arguments only brought to a head a long process of reconsideration. Even in 1538 he seems to have approved the teaching of Adam Damplip of Calais,[6] who asserted the real

---

1. P.S., I, pp. 391 f.; probably through Jewel, who seems to have acted as one of the notaries.
2. P.S., II, pp. 217-218.
3. P.S., II, p. 218.
4. P.S., II, pp. 342-343.
5. P.S., II, p. 218.
6. P.S., II, p. 375.

presence but did not accept the doctrine of transubstantiation. His own estimate is probably true: "By little and little I put away my former ignorance"; first abandoning transubstantiation and finally the real presence.[7] In the formulation of his new doctrine Ridley played a critical part, but so too did Peter Martyr,[8] to whom Cranmer was perhaps closer in spirit and outlook than any other continental reformer.

In relation to this doctrine, the first task of Cranmer as of all the reformers was necessarily negative. He had to oppose what he took to be a wrong doctrine of the eucharistic presence. In this field he had nothing very new to contribute. He simply repeated the main arguments of almost all the reformers, grouping them under his own threefold scheme of Scripture, the fathers and reason. He had three scriptural objections to transubstantiation and the related doctrine of the real presence: first, that the body of Christ is now in heaven, and will not return until the last day; second, that the discourse in John 6 speaks plainly of a spiritual and not a literal feeding; and third, that there are many parallels in both the Old and the New Testaments for a non-literal interpretation.[9] The fathers reinforced this line of thought, for Cranmer had a great list of patristic citations to prove the novelty of the medieval and contemporary teaching.[10] In this aspect of his work he was perhaps helped by Oecolampadius of Basle, who even in the twenties had made a special study of the patristic evidence. Ridley and Martyr were also well versed in the same field. But Cranmer had obviously consulted and weighed the passages for himself, and he discussed them with considerable perspicacity. Like Zwingli, he could also appeal sometimes to the *corpus iuris canonici*, which in places preserved the original catholic understanding in patristic citations and some of the earlier glosses.[11] A final argument was provided by reason, the main point here being that "the papistical doctrine is against all our outward senses, called our five wits".[12] When he said this he was not thinking rationalistically, for he admitted that

---

7. P.S., I, p. 374.
8. *Loc. cit.*
9. P.S., I, pp. 93 f.
10. P.S., I, pp. 94 f.
11. Cf. P.S., I, pp. 268, 281-282.
12. P.S., I, pp. 255-256.

"faith teacheth us to believe things that we see not".[13] Nor was he consciously a nominalist, for although the possibility of transubstantiation is easiest for a realist, not every realist will necessarily accept its reality. Cranmer's objection was not to the underlying distinction of substance and accident, but to the miraculous, or as he would call it magical divorce of the two. If a miracle is genuinely accomplished, and the body and blood of Christ replace the bread and wine, it ought to happen without any separation of substance and accidents, so that the body and blood of Christ can be seen and touched and tasted. The acts of God cannot be suspended on philosophical distinctions, however right and necessary these may be in their own sphere.

An elaboration of these points would fill a substantial volume, for they are argued in detail and with subtlety. But the negative aspect of Cranmer's teaching is not nearly so interesting or important as the positive. The question necessarily arises: Had Cranmer a genuine and consistent alternative to the rejected view? Even if the peculiar explanation of transubstantiation had to be rejected, could he find a satisfying doctrine of Christ's presence without in some form accepting a real or substantial presence? Had he a convincing interpretation of the action and words of Christ when he took bread and wine and said: "This is my body which is given for you"; "This is the new testament in my blood which is shed for you"?

Now Cranmer did not wish to deny a genuine presence of Jesus Christ in the eucharist. He did not think of the sacrament only as a symbol helping us to grasp a vague and generalized presence and therefore assisting our confidence in the goodness and redemptive love of God. Indeed, like his colleague Ridley he was willing enough to adopt and use the hotly disputed phrase "real presence" so long as it was not given a technical sense: "and yet this is really also (as you have expounded the word), that is to say, in deed and effectually".[14]

He put this very clearly in the so-called *Explication in Writing* which he drew up for the Oxford Disputation: "If ye understand by this word 'really', *re ipsa*, 'in very deed and effectually', so Christ, by grace and efficacy of his passion, is in deed and truly present

---

13. *Loc. cit.*   14. P.S., I, p. 71; cf. Ridley (P.S.), p. 196.

to all his true and holy members. But if ye understand by this word 'really', *corporaliter*, i.e., corporally, so that by the body of Christ is understood a natural body and organical, so the first proposition doth vary, not only from the usual speech and phrase of scripture, but also is clean contrary to the holy word of God and Christian profession."[15] In other words, Cranmer could not agree that Christ is present in the sacrament in the same way that He was present in the incarnation. But he did not oppose a true and actual presence: "and therefore you gather out of my sayings unjustly, that Christ is in deed absent; for I say (according to God's word and the doctrine of the old writers) that Christ is present in his sacraments, as they teach also that he is present in his word, when he worketh mightily by the same in the hearts of the hearers".[16] Or again: "We be agreed, as me seemeth, that Christ's body is present, and the same body that suffered."[17]

This true presence of Christ was not merely a presence after His deity, which Cranmer of course accepted like everyone else, and which we must not be tempted to underestimate. He quoted the words of Augustine in this connection: "Doubt not but our Lord Jesus Christ is everywhere present as God."[18] He also seemed to take it that the promises of Christ's general presence with His people indicated this presence after His deity, which is a very debatable point. The discussion as a whole suggests that at some stage in his thinking Cranmer had been tempted to think of the eucharistic presence primarily in terms of the divine nature, which would of course include the efficacy of the human. But if he succumbed in relation to the presence with the two or three, he resisted firmly and consistently, and very rightly, in relation to the sacramental presence, for as he said at his examination: "I believe, that whoso eateth and drinketh that sacrament, Christ is within them, whole Christ, his nativity, passion, resurrection and ascension."[19] To restrict the presence to the deity of Christ is to ignore the essential and critical element in the Gospel, that for our sake and for our salvation the Word became flesh, and

---

15. P.S., I, p. 395.
16. P.S., I, p. 11.
17. P.S., I, p. 91.
18. P.S., I, p. 94.
19. P.S., II, p. 213.

that the flesh was broken and the blood outpoured for us. A generalized divine presence is not enough. Indeed, in the light of the promise of the Paraclete it may be doubted whether this is the true interpretation of the presence to the two or three and to the disciples as a whole.

Rightly, however, Cranmer refused to bring in this human presence under cover of the divine, for he saw that this would necessarily involve a dangerous confusion of the natures. In this respect he is more perspicacious than Ridley, who seems to argue a presence of the body of Christ by virtue of His divine nature, although with the saving qualification that it is operative through God's word and sacraments.[20] Cranmer quoted Vigilius to the effect that "Christ is with us, and not with us, with us in the nature of his deity, and not with us in the nature of his humanity".[21] This argument was used by Vigilus, not to deny a true presence of Christ, but to overthrow the Eutychean heresy with its absorption of the human nature into the divine. Cranmer himself applied it in reverse, for he saw that to predicate the omnipresence of deity to Christ's humanity is to maintain a unity of nature: "they confound his two natures, his Godhead and his manhood, attributing unto his humanity that thing which appertaineth only to his divinity, that is to say, to be in heaven, earth, and in many places at one time."[22] On the other hand, if it is asserted that corporally Christ is both in heaven and in the bread and wine of innumerable communions, this is to "divide and separate his human nature or his body, making of one body of Christ two bodies and two natures".[23] Against this it may be argued, first, that it is difficult to say anything at all about Christ without disturbing the balance of unity and duality, and second, that Cranmer thinks of the presence of Christ in a rather crassly localized manner. But if we believe Christ genuinely to be the Word made flesh, the difficulties have to be accepted, and however we conceive Christ's presence in heaven, Cranmer is contending for a real truth, that Christ is not present on earth to-day in the same way as in His birth, life and crucifixion, and that the

---

20. Ridley (P.S.), p. 13.
21. P.S., I, p. 99.
22. P.S., I, p. 100.
23. *Loc. cit.*

distinction is not a distinction of human philosophy but of the divine economy.

So far, so good. But now Cranmer comes to the more difficult part of his thinking. He has said that Christ is indeed present in the supper, not merely after His deity, but in the body. He denies, however, that this is a substantial presence in the sense of a presence of his "natural body and organical".[24] The question therefore arises: What kind of a body is it? This is the core and centre of the matter, and although Cranmer expresses himself in different ways which sometimes suggest a slight confusion of understanding, there is no doubt at all as to his ultimate or basic meaning. His reply is twofold, reflecting again the incarnational duality which we find in his baptismal teaching.

First, to all those who receive the sacrament there is a figurative, or, preferably, a sacramental presence of Christ: "And although Christ in his human nature, substantially, really, corporally, naturally, and sensibly be present with his Father in heaven, yet sacramentally and spiritually he is here present. For in water, bread and wine he is present, as in signs and sacraments."[25] The argument here is that the bread and wine are signs, not merely to remind us of the incarnation and crucifixion of Jesus Christ, but to "bring them before us", to "exhibit" them in such a way that we can see and taste and handle, to give as it were a concrete although sacramental contemporaneity to the flesh and passion of the divine Son. In this sense, in the sign which is given the name of the thing signified, Christ is always present by the Holy Spirit, whether the sign is discerned and received in the Spirit or not discerned and not received. "For the diversity is not in the body, but in the eating thereof, no man eating it carnally; but the good eating it both sacramentally and spiritually, and the evil only sacramentally, that is, figuratively."[26]

This doctrine of a "sacramental" presence has several valuable features. It keeps the eucharistic action in line with the evangelical and baptismal, in which there is also a presentation, a making present of the incarnate and crucified Christ

---

24. P.S., I, p. 395.   25. P.S., I, p. 47.   26. P.S., I, p. 224.

by the Holy Spirit through the appointed means of grace. It preserves the proper analogy of incarnational duality, for whatever unity there may be, the sign has to be held distinct from the thing signified. It also keeps the pattern of what has sometimes been called the divine incognito in the flesh. Just as it was possible for men to see and hear Christ as the divine Son present in the flesh, yet not to know Him in His divine nature, so it is possible to see and receive the bread and wine, yet not to discern the body and blood of Christ exhibited and presented. If there is a legitimate criticism of Cranmer's exposition, it is perhaps that he makes the distinction too harsh. He does not seem to agree that Christ can be present in fact by the Spirit and sacrament, and not merely in figure, where there is no faithful reception. He accepts the duality of the natures of the sacrament, but not a true unity of the "person". He is quite open about this: "For the two natures of Christ be joined together in unity of person, which unity is not between the sacrament and the body of Christ."[27] In a sense, of course, he is right, for such unity as there is is only analogous, and it is not a natural or organic unity but a unity by the Holy Spirit. All the same, he does not sufficiently emphasize that it is a real and even an objective unity. In the sacrament as in the word Christ is always proffered or presented, whether or not He is recognized and known. From this point of view we can speak of Him as objectively present by the Spirit in every administration of the sacrament. But subjectively, in the eating or reception, the presence will be only sacramental where there is no discernment of the Lord's body, where the elements are not taken in the Spirit and therefore in faith.

If this had been all Cranmer's teaching, he might perhaps have come under the charge of a bare memorialism or symbolism, for with a subjective reference the bread and wine are no more than external signs to those who receive without faith. But where this is the case, the fault is really in the recipient, so that even as a sign the sacrament is rather more than an ordinary pictorial re-enactment. This point comes out very clearly when Cranmer discusses the so-called spiritual presence

---

27. P.S., I, p. 284.

of Christ which is added to the sacramental or figurative presence when the sacrament is rightly received. This spiritual presence is something much deeper and fuller than anything we meet with in a pure memorialism. It is the real presence of Christ as Cranmer understood it. But it is a real presence, not in the elements as such, but in the reception of the elements in true and inward faith.

A first point to remember is that when Cranmer uses the word "spiritual" he does not mean by it the rather nebulous thing that we so often associate with the word to-day. The context of his thought is not Gnostic or Manichean but biblical. His concern is to bring out the genuine New Testament distinction between the mode of Christ's presence incarnate and the mode of His presence resurrected and ascended. It is the same Christ who is present. But in the one case He is present in the body, in the other in the spirit; or, to put it another way, by and in the Holy Spirit. As he says himself in the preface: "Christ and his Holy Spirit be truly and indeed present."[28]

There is the lesser but not unimportant point that the presence is not in the elements as such but in their due administration according to Christ's ordinance and institution. The same could be said of the sacramental presence, for the whole point of this sign is that it is an action. The bread and wine alone do not constitute the sign, but the bread and wine broken, poured out and received. The stress on reception obviously carries with it a danger of subjectivization which Cranmer does not wholly escape. We can agree that in contradistinction to the word – at any rate the word written – the sacrament does not exist except where it is administered. But that does not mean that it is necessarily more subjective. The word, too, has to be read and proclaimed and spiritually received. The sacrament when it is administered can still be an objective sign by the Holy Ghost, so that Christ is always attested and presented, even if not received by this or that individual. Where Cranmer is right is that there is no "presentation" in the static element: hence a legitimate objection to the adoration of reserved bread and wine.

---

28. P.S., I, p. 3.

A third point in Cranmer's treatment is the tremendous emphasis which he again lays on faith. The presence of Jesus Christ subjectively in the Spirit means His presence to faith or to the faithful recipient. Cranmer underlines this again and again and in all kinds of ways. He cannot allow that "evil men do eat the very body and drink the very blood of Christ".[29] He finds the true or spiritual presence of Christ only "in them that worthily receive the outward sacrament".[30] The effect of the sacrament, as we shall see in the next chapter, is only to those who have faith, for it is they alone who can see through the external element to the internal reality, and therefore enjoy the benefit of Christ's presence. Faith is the means by which the Lord's body is discerned and profitably received, just as it is the means by which the Lord Christ is perceived and accepted in the man Jesus. Again, Cranmer maintains the personal nature of faith as against those who argued that Augustine's "Believe, and thou hast eaten"[31] referred only to a belief that the bread is His body. "This spiritual presence of Christ is to the man who putteth his whole hope and trust of his redemption and salvation in that only sacrifice which Christ made upon the cross."[32] Indeed, the rejection of transubstantiation is a general plea for faith, for transubstantiation involves an attempt to have Christ in a direct and accessible manner, by sight and not by faith and the Spirit. Nor is it only a question of knowledge, for our entry into Jesus Christ in His being and work for us, and our whole life in Him, are not visible and perceptible, but by the Holy Spirit and therefore again in faith.

This is all very true, and the emphasis must be maintained at all costs. But it must not be maintained in such a way that access is given at once to the threatened subjectivization. Carried to extremes, the doctrine that there is a presence only to faith means that the presence of Jesus Christ is suspended on the presence of faith at the time of reception, that there is no presence at all except to the faithful recipient. Cranmer himself does not really say this, for his distinction between the sacramental and the spiritual is only a subjective distinction

---

29. P.S., I, p. 13.
30. P.S., I, pp. 3, 55, etc.
31. *Cf.* P.S., I, p. 208.
32. P.S., I, p. 207.

which does not necessarily affect an objective presentation of Christ by the Spirit. As we have quoted before: "The diversity is not in the body, but in the eating thereof."[33] On the other hand, Cranmer virtually ignores any objective presence, and his suggestion is that Christ is not present at all (or only in sign) except when He is received. But is this a true or balanced account? The examples of the incarnation and the word will perhaps be a help to us. In the actual encounters between men and the incarnate Christ or the Gospel of Christ the response varies. There are some who in faith recognize the divine Son or the life-giving word, and in faithful reception they know the divine power and presence. But on the other hand, and sometimes on the very same occasions, there are those who do not. Yet we can still say, and we still have to say, that Christ Himself is still present or presented in the flesh or in His word. Objectively, He is there, although in this or that individual case He may be received only as a man or His Gospel as a human opinion, and there is therefore no subjective presence. Now in the same way Jesus Christ is objectively present in the sacramental encounter, although this objective presence does not find its subjective response or fulfilment except where there is faith. The importance of faith is obviously in relation to the subjective apprehension of the presence. Cranmer is therefore quite right when he says: "He is received in the heart, and entereth in by faith."[34] He is also right in his strong emphasis on this aspect, for, after all, the subjective apprehension is the goal and objective of the evangelical and sacramental encounter. He ignores, perhaps, the final safeguard against subjectivizing, the objective presence of Christ by the Spirit, but he maintains always the no less effective safeguard that faith itself is reception in the Holy Spirit. The operation of the Holy Spirit is the underlying truth in every form of eucharistic objectivization. Indeed, we can go further. Without a proper appreciation of the Holy Spirit and His work, the subjective and the objective aspects can never be justly assessed or correctly related and understood.

The final point in Cranmer's survey is that the Christ who is

---

33. P.S., I, p. 224.   34. P.S., I, p. 57.

sacramentally or spiritually present is not merely the incarnate but the crucified and risen Christ. He puts this most plainly in the examination: "I believe that Christ is within them, whole Christ, his nativity, passion, resurrection, and ascension, but not that corporally that sitteth in heaven."[35] Again, in his exposition he made it plain that the Lord's supper is not merely a sacrament of the body and blood of Christ, but that it is a sacrament of the broken body and the outpoured blood. The food which Christ gave was not only His humanity, but His crucified humanity: "For there is no kind of meat that is comfortable to the soul, but only the death of Christ's blessed body; *nor* no kind of drink that can quench her thirst, but only the bloodshedding of our saviour Christ, which is shed for her offences."[36] The eucharistic food is not the food only of Christ incarnate sanctifying human life, but of Christ crucified and risen, destroying the old life of sin, and giving the new life of righteousness.

Now we have already touched on the same point in relation to the mode of Christ's presence. He is not now present as incarnate, but crucified, resurrected and ascended He is present by the Spirit. When we say this, however, it is not simply a question of inter-trinitarian economics. It takes us to the very heart of the Gospel which is the record of the redemptive work of God in Jesus Christ. The incarnation of Jesus Christ cannot be divorced from His atonement. There is no simple solution of the human problem, the problem of sin and the consequent estrangement of God, merely by an organic conjunction of the divine and the human. Jesus Christ took flesh in order to die in the flesh. He made Himself one with us in order to take to Himself representatively the judgment of God on our flesh, in order to bring to an end our present life in the flesh and to replace it by a new life which begins in the Spirit, the life of the resurrection which in this world is always a life of faith in Jesus Christ. If the sacrament does attest an organic union between Christ's flesh and ours, it is to tell us that by virtue of that union our life in the flesh is judged, destroyed, and ended. But Christ as our representative has also been raised

---

35. P.S., II, p. 213.   36. P.S., I, p. 40.

again in the flesh. The sacrament, therefore, attests that our true and only life is the new, eternal life which we have in Christ, not organically, for we are not yet raised in the body, but by the Spirit and in faith. That is why Cranmer can always find an eschatological reference in the sacrament. It has a forward look, not only to the coming of Christ, but to the fulfilment of our new life in Him: "So is every good Christian spiritually born unto eternal life."[37] The statement that Christ took our life in order to give us His life is true enough in itself, but it is an abbreviated truth. It is, therefore, true only when we remember that He laid down His life in order to take it again. The saving union with Christ is the union with Christ crucified and risen.

The fact that the Christ present in the sacrament is crucified and risen and not merely incarnate explains the difference which Cranmer sees between the incarnation and sacrament. It is also his answer to the apparent contradiction which some scholars have seen in his teaching.[38] The point emerges most clearly in the discussion of a disputed passage in Hilary.[39] Whether or not Cranmer is giving a correct interpretation of Hilary does not affect the issue. What matters is that he is undoubtedly giving a correct interpretation of the Gospel. He agrees with Hilary that "Christ dwelleth in us by his incarnation", and therefore that he may be said to dwell in us "by receiving of our mortal nature".[40] This can be called a substantial or organic union, both as it affects Christ Himself in His divine-human life, and also as it affects the incarnate Christ in His relation to man. He also agrees with Hilary that Christ enables us to partake of His own immortality or eternal life.[41] This, too, will be a substantial or organic union, although in the first instance it will not be a simple union of man with God but a union of man with the God-man. And there are two very important features of this latter union. For one thing, it is not merely by virtue of the incarnation, but by virtue of the

---

37. P.S., I, p. 40.
38. Cf. C.C. Richardson : *Cranmer dixit et contradixit*, pp. 39 f.
39. P.S., I, pp. 160 f.
40. P.S., I, p. 165.
41. *Loc. cit.*

crucifixion and resurrection. Christ united Himself with our mortal flesh in order to die in the flesh and to be raised again in newness of life. The union of the Christian with Christ is an identification with Him in the death of the old man and the raising again of the new. Second, the union will one day be substantial and organic, but this is not so for the moment. If it were, there would be no need of the sacrament at all. During life in this world it is a union of faith in which we do not know Christ after the flesh but by the Spirit: beyond Golgotha and even Olivet. St. Paul put it in this way: "The life which I now live I live by the faith of the Son of God, who loved me and gave himself for me."

At bottom, therefore, the supposed inconsistency of Cranmer is a loyalty to the representative work of Christ in atonement. There is no organic union of life merely by virtue of incarnation. That is far too simple to be true. It makes nonsense of the very cross which we show forth. The only organic union is a union to death. Between the ascension and the last day there can be no direct union in the body. How can there be when this is a body of death? when we are to be raised in a new body? when in this body we walk by faith and not by sight? Christ has indeed taken our flesh. He has died in the flesh. He has risen and ascended in the new flesh to a life which is now our true life and which in the resurrection we shall have with Him. In the time of the church the word is given to the world and the sacrament is given to the church to attest the "now" of God in Jesus Christ which is received in faith but is still a "not yet" for man: "It doth not yet appear what we shall be: but we know that, when he shall appear, we shall be like him; for we shall see him as he is" (1 John 3:2).

In all fairness, we have to admit that Cranmer does not develop all these insights himself. He becomes so enmeshed in the detailed refutation of a false teaching that he cannot work out the implications of all his positive statements. He is also hampered continually by the fear that what he says will be snatched on by his opponents as concessions or admissions which finally prove their view. Perhaps the most surprising thing is that he does not consider much more closely the doctrine of the representative work of Christ in its bearing on the sacrament. He has a prior concern for this work. He obviously assumes it, as we see from his many references and his plain assertion that it is the whole Christ who is sacramentally or spiritually present in communion. But it deserves a fuller consideration, for if this point is not clear everything else will be blurred or distorted. In the light of this work and with some slight shifts of terminology and emphasis, the teaching of Cranmer will still give us the most satisfying account of the eucharistic presence.

We can sum it up in this way. It is a presence of Jesus Christ who became flesh with us, who in the flesh suffered the death which is the judgment of the flesh, who on our behalf was raised to the new life which is our true life in the new body with which we shall one day be clothed. It is a presence of this incarnate, crucified, risen and ascended Christ by the Holy Spirit through the mediacy of appointed word and signs. The office of the Holy Spirit is not merely to give us a symbolic reminder of Christ's person and work, but to make Him our contemporary, so that in the signs we are genuinely confronted with Christ and His redemption. Objectively – to replace Cranmer's "sacramentally" – this is always a real presence, for all those who receive the sign are confronted with Christ Himself incarnate, crucified and risen for them. But subjectively – Cranmer's "inwardly and spiritually" – it is a real presence only to those who receive in faith, for it is in faith that the witness and work of the Spirit is fulfilled and there is personal entry into Christ's saving work. In the Spirit believers have a two-way enjoyment of Christ's presence. Jesus. Christ has come to them. They discern the Lord's body as it was given for them: "Consider and behold my body crucified for you. Chaw you upon my passion, be fed with my death."[42] But they are also lifted up to Jesus Christ, where their true life is hid with Christ in God: "that being like eagles in this life, we should fly up to heaven in our hearts, where that lamb is resident at the right hand of his Father, which taketh away the sins of the world."[43]

---

42. P.S., I, p. 399. 43. P.S., I, p.398.

The weakness in all other interpretations is that they do not take into account a presence of the "whole Christ", An emphasis on the organic union by incarnation minimizes, ignores or evades the purpose and outworking of this union in the cross and resurrection. This error was at least partially avoided in the Middle Ages with its stark and almost brutal re-enactment of the passion. But an emphasis on the substantial presence of Christ crucified forgets that the Christ who died is now risen, ascended and glorified, so that when He comes, it is as He came to the divine who was in the Spirit on the Lord's Day. The incarnation cannot be isolated from the crucifixion, but again, the crucifixion cannot be isolated from the resurrection and ascension, which also mean Pentecost. No account can be satisfactory which does not do justice to the fact that it is the whole Christ who is present. But between the ascension and the parousia, which is the time of word and sacrament ("until he come"), this means that it is necessarily a presence by the Holy Spirit. Therefore no account can be satisfactory which does not do justice to the fact and mission of the Holy Spirit in relation to Jesus Christ. As we have said before, it is not enough to be incarnational. Christology and soteriology belong together, and they both involve pneumatology. We may not be able to accept all the details of Cranmer's teaching or terminology. But it is the merit of his doctrine of the presence that these basic and indispensable truths are everywhere recognized and respected.

7
The Eucharistic Work

There is obviously a close connection between Christ's presence in the sacrament and His work in the sacrament. This appears in the traditionalist teaching, for hand in hand with the doctrine of a substantial presence there went the twofold idea of a re-enactment of the sacrifice of Christ and a nourishment of the Christian by corporal reception. The first work was, of course, purely objective in the sense that it took place independently of the state or even the presence of recipients. The second was also objective to the extent that all who receive the sacrament receive the body of Christ, but all the same it is subjective too in the sense that only the worthy recipients enjoy the sacramental benefit.

The rejection of the first part of this twofold work came quite early in Cranmer's career of reform, and it seems to be related to his repudiation of the narrower doctrine of transubstantiation (as opposed to a real presence). Some questions were put to the bishops on this matter in 1547, and in his own answer Cranmer stated clearly that the private mass cannot be of any value except to the administrator,[1] and that "the oblation and sacrifice of Christ in the mass is not so called, because Christ indeed is there offered and sacrificed by the priest and the people (for that was done but once by himself upon the cross), but it is so called because it is a memory and representation of that very true sacrifice and immolation which before was made upon the cross".[2] He did not, therefore, think it "convenient" that satisfactory masses should continue.

To put it bluntly, Cranmer could not accept the notion that there is an actual immolation of Christ on an altar. Nor did he think that anything can be added to the sole-sufficiency of Christ's atoning work, even in respect of the lesser penalties of post-baptismal sin. This was the primary reason why so soon

---

1. P.S., II, p. 150. 2. P.S., II, p. 151.

afterwards it was ordered that "the Lord's board should rather be after the form of a table than of an altar".[3] "For the use of an altar is to make sacrifice upon it: the use of a table is to serve for men to eat upon. Now when we come unto the Lord's board, what do we come for? To sacrifice Christ again, and to crucify him again; or to feed upon him that was once only crucified and offered up for us?"[4] The change received official authorization in the 1552 revision.

In his treatise on the Lord's supper Cranmer took up the same question in his fifth book *Of the Oblation and Satisfaction of Christ*. His first concern was for the glory of Jesus Christ and the fulness of His atoning work. For the uniqueness of the propitiatory sacrifice of Christ he found many passages, especially in the epistle to the Hebrews. In this priestly office "he admitteth neither partner nor successor. For by his own oblation he satisfieth his Father for all men's sins, and reconciled mankind unto his grace and favour."[5] The result is that if there is a re-offering of Christ on the sacramental altar, an attempt is made by human priests to add in some way to the one sacrifice of Christ, or else there is a continual repetition of the "wicked act" of the "wicked Jews and Pharisees".[6] Either way, injury is done to Jesus Christ Himself. The scriptural evidence is supported by the patristic,[7] for although, as Cranmer allows, the fathers often speak of communion as a sacrifice they do so only because "it is a sign or representation of the true sacrifice".[8] Lombard himself "judged truly in this point, saying: 'That which is offered and consecrated of the priest is called a sacrifice and oblation, because it is a memory and representation of the true sacrifice and holy oblation made in the altar of the cross.'"[9]

We need not labour the point, for to-day the singularity of Christ's work of reconciliation is an integral part of the Protestant heritage. Even those who like to speak of an altar and prefer to say re-presentation rather than representation would hesitate to ascribe a full-blooded propitiatory value to the

---

3. P.S., II, pp. 524-525.
4. P.S., II, p. 525.
5. P.S., I, p. 346.
6. P.S., I, p. 348.
7. P.S., I, pp. 351 f.
8. *Loc. cit.*
9. P.S., I, p. 351.

"mass," or to see in it a literal immolation of the body and blood of Christ. The Bible teaches and the Gospel itself demands a uniqueness of Jesus Christ and His work, so that whatever concessions may be made to medieval thinking and language, it is recognized that the very idea of a supplementary or repetitive offering, even for the temporal penalties of post-baptismal sin, is quite foreign to the evangelical message. If this is not recognized, the doctrine opposed by Cranmer and all reformers is of course the logical alternative.

The question arises, however, whether the terms "memory and representation" are quite strong enough for this more strictly objective aspect of the eucharistic work. The supper is obviously a memorial or remembrance, for Jesus Christ Himself said: "This do in remembrance of me." It is also a representation, for as Paul said: "Ye do shew the Lord's death." But as Cranmer understood this, it does not seem to amount to very much more than a figurative or symbolical re-enactment. Ought we not to think of the representation as something very much more concrete in accordance with a more objective conception of the presence? Is it not the case that in and through this sign the Holy Spirit does actually present to us the Christ once crucified for our sin, or, to put it another way, He brings us into the presence of Christ crucified, confronting us with the cup of judgment and salvation which Jesus did not refuse in Gethsemane?

The point is not, of course, that we present or plead the sacrifice before God as a ground of acceptance. There is a grain of truth in this, as there is in the similar view of pleading the divine promises. But word and sacrament were given primarily, not as a reminder to God, but as a guarantee to us. It is not that we hold out to God a ground of acceptance but that God holds out to us a ground of assurance. Again, the work of the Holy Spirit is not in any sense to make Christ present to God, for incarnate, crucified and risen, Christ is at the right hand of the Father. The work of the Holy Spirit is to make Him present to us, so that we are confronted with His cross and passion as an event for us. When we take and receive the elements in obedience to His command, the sacrifice of Christ is not repeated, but there is more than a symbolical representation. In the Spirit we are in the presence of that one sacrifice for sins for ever which is the true eucharistic as it is also the true baptismal work. If it is a memory or representation, it is in this deep sense which in the last resort is the mystery of the Holy Ghost. Cranmer himself did not and could not bring out the fulness of this objective aspect, but he certainly emphasized to the best of his ability the actuality of the event remembered: "The priest should declare the death and passion of Christ, and all the people should look upon the cross in the mount of Calvary, and see Christ there hanging, and the blood flowing out of his side into their wounds to heal all their sores; and the priest and people all together should laud and thank instantly the chirurgeon and physician of their souls. And this is the priest's and people's sacrifice, not to be propitiators for sin, but (as Emissene saith) to worship continually in mystery that which was but once offered for the price of sin."[10] As always in the sacrament, it will be seen that this strictly objective work has at once a subjective reference and application.

But there is also a more definitely subjective side which Cranmer develops with great power. For if it is the office of the sacrament to bring before us the sacrifice of Christ, its sacrificial work includes not only the application of that work, but the response of self-offering to Christ which is evoked by that sacrifice and demanded of all the recipients. In the first instance this response is a sacrifice of "laud and praise",[11] for it is a grateful recognition of the saving work of Christ. It is also a sacrifice of repentance and obedience, for "trusting to have remission of sins, and to be delivered from eternal death and hell, by the merit only of the death and blood of Christ, we must kill devilish pride, furious anger, insatiable covetousness, filthy lucre, stinking lechery, deadly hatred and malice, foxy wiliness, wolfish ravening and devouring, and all other unreasonable desires and lusts of the flesh. And as many as belong to Christ must crucify and kill these for Christ's sake, as Christ crucified himself for us."[12]

---

10. P.S., I, p. 359.   11. P.S., I, p. 352.   12. P.S., I, p. 349.

At a first glance, it seems that we have here a thoroughgoing subjectivization of the eucharistic sacrifice. It is the sacrifice of the Christian to God, not the sacrifice of God for the Christian. But as we can see even from the Prayer Book revision of 1552, Cranmer does not give to this subjective sacrifice an autonomous or even a primary significance. It is a sacrifice only on the basis of the represented sacrifice of Jesus Christ, and as a response to it. What takes place in communion is not merely that we offer ourselves to God, but that we offer ourselves to God in answer to the remembered self-offering of God for us. If there is a subjectivist trend in Cranmer's thinking, it starts further back. He does not give sufficient concretion to the sacramental representation. It tends to become a mental or emotional recollection evoked by the sacramental symbols. Even so, however, it does always have reference to the real work of Jesus Christ at Calvary, and it is a recollection in the Holy Spirit. It is never a mental construction pure and simple. In this sense Jesus Christ and His redemptive work for us are always "exhibited" to recipients, and it is by way of appropriation and response, not as an independent or initiatory act, that there is the sacrifice of thanksgiving and discipleship.

But even if that is the case, we may still ask whether it is a true account of the sacrament, that its sacrificial work consists mostly in the self-offering of believing recipients. There can be no doubt, of course, that from a very early time this effect has been associated with the eucharist. Almost always the liturgies have included a sacrificial response on the part of the congregation. The passion of Christ cannot be contemplated in faith without producing a movement of this kind. Self-offering is certainly a by-product of the sacramental action. But is it the work itself? The eucharistic passages in the New Testament do not say so, but it seems a legitimate deduction from New Testament teaching. If the objective work attested by word and sacrament is the representative action of Jesus Christ, the subjective work effected by word and sacrament is the appropriation which means identification with Jesus Christ in His crucifixion and resurrection. In this respect the Lord's supper continues the work of baptism. In baptism as an initiatory sacrament the emphasis falls on the primary identification, but with a view to mortification and renewal and ultimately to dissolution and resurrection. In the Lord's supper the emphasis is on the life-long identification in discipleship, but with a backward look to conversion and a forward look to the final consummation, To accomplish or at least to further the response of self-dedication is undoubtedly a very important effect of the sacrament.

All the same, we have to recognize that in the first instance this is the baptismal rather than the eucharistic work. The sacraments cannot be artificially divided. They obviously belong together. The saving action of Jesus Christ is at one and the same time the true baptism and the true cup. In the objective which is the primary sphere the sacraments proclaim the same message. They are the sacraments of Jesus Christ in His death and resurrection. But each sacrament has its own function and therefore its own emphasis, especially in its relevance for us, that is to say, the subjective side. The aspect of self-identification, the ending of the old life and the entry into the new, is particularly stressed in baptism. In communion the main emphasis falls on the nourishing and strengthening of the new life by feeding on Christ crucified and risen who is Himself the true life of Christians both individually and corporately. This is not a theme apart, for the strengthening of the new life means in effect the putting off of the old and the putting on of the new, which is the very essence of self-offering. But it is a theme in which the dominant motif is not the sacrificial response as such, but that response as a committal to Jesus Christ, or even a receiving of Jesus Christ, as Himself the source of nourishment and life.

Cranmer has, of course, a great deal to say about this aspect. We remember his awareness of the point in his insistence that the Lord's board is a table: "Now when we come unto the Lord's table, what do we come for? To sacrifice him again, and to crucify him again; or to feed upon him that was once only crucified and offered up for us?"[13] Again, in his work on the *True and Catholic Doctrine* he devotes a whole book to

---

13. P.S., II, p. 525.

The Eating and Drinking.[14] The Christ whose flesh and blood are present by the Spirit is the Christ who was once crucified for sin, who is raised again in newness of life, and who gives Himself to us, nourishing and in that way preserving our bodies and souls to eternal life as He Himself promised in the great discourse of John 6.[15] Nor is the nourishing and strengthening only an individual matter. Cranmer is particularly insistent that if our fellowship is with Him it is also with one another. Christ is the life of individual Christians but He is also the life of the church which is His body. In the communion, therefore, Christians are nourished and strengthened together as the one body in Jesus Christ. Individually, "every good christian man is spiritually fed and nourished in his soul by the flesh and blood of our Saviour Christ" who "preserveth both body and soul for ever".[16] Corporately, "all faithful Christians be spiritually turned into the body of Christ, and so be joined unto Christ, and also together among themselves, that they do make but one mystical body of Christ, as St. Paul saith: 'We be one bread and one body, as many as be partakers of one bread and one cup'."[17]

When he comes to the detailed discussion, Cranmer has to combat two misleading doctrines which he found in traditionalist teaching. The first concerns the nature of the eating, which was commonly asserted to be "carnal": "The gross error of the papists is of the carnal eating and drinking of Christ's flesh and blood with our mouths".[18] Like Zwingli, Cranmer finds a crass and almost cannibalistic literalism in the recantation enforced on Berengarius: "that we do actually chaw and tear in pieces with the teeth".[19] He identifies this doctrine with the so-called Capernaitic error of John 6. In a strict sense, of course, the carnal eating is substantial rather than cannibalistic, but this is a distinction which can be carried through only in non-biblical categories. Cranmer's own point is simple enough.

There is a genuine partaking of the flesh and blood of Jesus Christ, but not with the mouth, and not of the flesh and blood as they were present in the upper room and given for us on the

---

14. P.S., I, pp. 201 f. 16. P.S., I, p. 40. 18. P.S., I, p. 207.
15. P.S., I, p. 40. 17. P.S., I, p. 42. 19. P.S., I, p. 203.

cross.[20] As with the presence itself, Cranmer's distinction is not in terms of philosophy but in terms of the divine economy as revealed in the Bible. It is in the Holy Spirit that we feed upon the body and blood of the incarnate, crucified, risen and ascended Christ who is now made present to us by the Spirit. This leads Cranmer to the complementary thought that not all those who receive the bread and wine are nourished with the body and blood of Christ to eternal life and fellowship in the body.[21] On a carnal or substantial view of the eating it is impossible to deny that the wicked do in fact partake of the body and blood of Christ. Gardiner has to recognize, of course, that there is a distinction between the eating of the wicked, which is sacramental only and to condemnation, and the eating of those who receive the sacrament "with a true sincere charitable faith", which is both sacramental and spiritual.[22] But although he uses the same terms as Cranmer, the fact remains that all of them receive the actual body and blood, the wicked to spiritual hurt, the good to spiritual profit. Cranmer made exactly the same distinction between sacramental and spiritual receiving, but he drew the line in a different way, or perhaps we ought to say, at a different place. Only the good receive the body and blood of Jesus Christ. The wicked receive the sign but they do not have the thing signified. Perhaps we can put it in this way. As Gardiner sees it, all receive the nourishment by external participation, but all do not have the nourishing. As Cranmer sees it, the nourishment is held out to all, and all receive the sign of it. But only the faithful have both nourishment and nourishing.

Cranmer's positive doctrine of eating and drinking as the main work of the sacrament conforms to the common pattern of his sacramental understanding, and it has therefore the same strength and the same weakness. It can be summarized in this way. In the Lord's supper as in baptism Jesus Christ is present by the Holy Spirit, offering Himself as the life and nourishment of the Christian and the Christian church. Only in faith, however, is this presence of Christ perceived and therefore operative, so that the unbeliever knows and receives only the external

---

20. Cf. P.S., I, p. 46.   21. P.S., I, pp. 207 f.   22. P.S., I, p. 201.

sign and does not enjoy the health-giving properties either in his own life or in the life of the church. To talk of any other kind of bodily reception is to oppose the clear teaching of John 6, to misinterpret the fathers, and to confuse the sign with the thing signified. The weakness of Cranmer's view, as Gardiner himself pointed out, is that in some sense Christ is still the nourishment even of the unbeliever, although he is not in fact perceived and enjoyed as such. The Christ who is proffered in the sacrament is no less the Christ who is our life and nourishment because we refuse to accept him as such. To say otherwise is to deny what is the very heart of the faith: the representative work of Jesus Christ in His incarnation, crucifixion, resurrection, and ascension. Now at bottom Cranmer did not wish to deny this, but with his (enforced) stress on the subjective aspect, and in his anxiety not to suggest a carnal participation, he came perilously near to jeopardizing it. The separation between sign and thing signified had to be made, but it was made rather too harshly and with no express appreciation of the underlying unity.

That is the one side. But as against that, we must remember that by its very nature participation is a positively subjective act, so that it is very difficult to think of an objective participation irrespective of reception. Certainly, an objective life and nourishment is always held out to all in Jesus Christ. Cranmer would not deny this. But even as opposed to baptism, communion is actively subjective. We have not merely to be nourished as we are baptized. We have to take and eat. Therefore the emphasis in relation to the effect or work has to have a markedly subjective character. Jesus Christ is held out as the life and nourishment of all participants. They all receive the sign of the proffered nourishment. But even on the traditionalist view not all are actually nourished. The only point at issue, therefore, is whether or not the wicked (who are not nourished) do actually receive the nourishment. If so, that means that not merely the sacrament but the actual body of Christ is received in vain and even to condemnation: an idea which Cranmer cannot accept and which is not sustained by the wording of the relevant passaged in I Corinthians II. The most that can be said is that by the Holy Spirit the nourishment is always there. But where there is no inward nourishing there is no receiving of nourishment. To be fed by Christ is to feed on Christ. To feed on Christ is to receive Him in an individual act of faith. Without this act of receiving there can be no participation in Christ, but only in the outward sign. This distinction has to be made between feeding in sign and feeding in inward truth, even though there is in fact an underlying unity, that Christ Himself is held out as the bread of life. The distinction, as Cranmer would say, is in the eating. To fail to see this is to destroy the nature of a sacrament and to misunderstand, although not of course to deny, the critical importance of subjective participation.

Again, it is a strong point in Cranmer's analysis that effective feeding upon Christ is described as spiritual rather than carnal or substantial. Even Gardiner had spoken of effective participation as spiritual, and Cranmer commended this analysis: "This your noting is very true, if it be truly understand."[23] But as Cranmer understood it, it meant that Christ Himself is received only in a spiritual way because the body and blood of Christ crucified, risen and ascended are present only by the Holy Spirit. Therefore the wicked who receive the sacrament without faith and apart from the Spirit receive Him only in sign, i.e., sacramentally as Cranmer uses the term. We have considered this aspect in relation to the presence of Christ and it need not be laboured again. It works two ways. Christ Himself is present and proffered by the Spirit. But faithful reception is also in the Spirit. Full justice is therefore done to the office and ministry of the Holy Spirit, as is not really possible on the postulate of a substantial presence and participation.

But the participation is also spiritual in the sense that it has to do with the new life of the spirit rather than the old and passing life of the flesh. At this point we must be careful not to read into Cranmer's usage the non-biblical categories of a spiritualizing which denies the body altogether. Cranmer's distinction between a carnal and spiritual nourishment is the

---

23. P.S., I, p. 205.

distinction between a nourishment of this present life which is sentenced and judged and destroyed in Jesus Christ and the nourishment of the new and resurrection life which has been given in Jesus Christ and will be fulfilled at the last day. The new life, too, is to be a life in the body. Therefore Cranmer insists upon the preservation of body and soul to eternal life. But it is in fact a new life which in this world we know only in the Spirit and by faith: "and not only they, but ourselves also, which have the first-fruits of the Spirit, even we ourselves groan within ourselves, waiting for the adoption, to wit, the redemption of our body." A carnal nourishment of this present body would be of no profit, for Christ is the bread of eternal life and therefore of the new life in the Spirit. A true partaking of Christ is therefore a reception in the Spirit of Christ present by the Spirit. The sign itself, like the baptismal sign, is given for the time between the ascension and the parousia, the time of the mortifying of the old life and the nourishment of the new. It is the means of Christ's presence by the Spirit. At the parousia it will no longer be necessary, for then Christ will be the life of Christians and the Christian church, not only representatively and by faith, but in resurrection fulness.

In this context we can again appreciate the importance of faith for a conjunction of sign and thing signified, and therefore for effective participation. Gardiner, too, was willing to give a prominent place to "charitable faith". He could not do otherwise, for in the great discourse of John 6 feeding is plainly linked with believing, and many fathers had stressed the necessity for reception in faith. On every interpretation faith had a critical significance. Without it, reception of the sacrament was plainly to condemnation. But for Cranmer, faith meant a difference between the receiving only of the elements and the receiving of Christ. He argued it out in this way. Christ Himself cannot be a bread of death, but only of life. The word and sacrament can be life to some and death to others, for some will receive them with faith and some in unbelief. But Christ cannot Himself be received except in faith and He is always the bread of life nourishing to eternity. If we have faith, therefore, we receive not only the word and sacrament but also

Christ Himself and life and nourishment in Christ. If we do not have faith, we do not even discern Christ, let alone receive Him, and the sign of His body and blood is taken to our condemnation.

Does this mean that the effect of the sacrament is subjectively suspended? Up to a point, this is undoubtedly Cranmer's view. Objectively, of course, Christ is still the nourishment of all men, but obviously a subjective participation has to be subjectively suspended. We cannot feed upon Christ except where we receive Him, and we cannot receive Him except in the subjective act which outwardly is taking and inwardly is faith. From this point of view faith is indispensable to the individual and corporate efficacy of the sacrament. Indeed, faith enters in at every point. It is confirmed by the contemporaneity of Christ in His redemptive action. This is part of the eucharistic strengthening. It is a principle of the new life which is sustained as faith itself is augmented: for the life of the Christian is a life of faith. Without faith there is no Christian life, and without faith there can be no nourishing of that life. Faith is indeed the eating, and the eating faith, as in the famous dictum of Augustine: "Believe, and thou hast eaten." To that extent a subjective suspension is unavoidable; for it belongs to the very essence of the matter. But it is a subjective suspension only in the self-evident and almost tautological way that faith is not a condition of the work, but is itself the work. To say that Christ cannot be received without faith is merely to say that He cannot be received without our receiving Him, or that we cannot be fed by Christ without feeding on Him. From the point of view of effective participation, we have to say and we can boldly say that although Christ and His saving work are the primary condition, faith itself is also indispensable.

And in the last resort even this is not a subjective suspension, for the faith in which Christians and the church are nourished to eternal life is not of human derivation but is itself the gift and work of the Word and Spirit. Faith is in fact evoked and strengthened by the word proclaimed and represented in the power of the Holy Ghost. That means that although faith is necessary it is never the first thing. Without it there is no subjective work, for it is itself the subjective work. It is, therefore, self-evidently indispensable. But it is not autonomous or self-derivative. The operation of the Holy Spirit, which is the true and ultimate pre-condition of effective participation, is not itself dependent upon a human pre-requisite. It is the Holy Spirit Himself who gives faith, and although the main purpose of the eucharistic nourishment is the development of the new life and therefore the strengthening of an existing faith, it is not impossible for the Holy Spirit to give life and faith even in and through the eucharistic word and administration. This cannot be presumed. It is not an excuse for unbelieving participation. But it underlines the fact that faith and the new life can neither exist nor be confirmed apart from the Spirit's attestation of Jesus Christ by word and sacrament. Faith always rests on the objective actuality of the atoning work of the Christ and the attesting work of the Spirit. If there is no faith, there is no work of the Spirit, and therefore no sacramental efficacy, not because the Spirit cannot work where there is no faith, but because where the Spirit does work, faith is always evoked or confirmed. What matters in the final analysis is the sovereign operation of the Holy Spirit Himself. This is not brought out too clearly in Cranmer's discussion of the eucharistic feeding, in which his main concern is to establish a plain distinction between worthy and unworthy reception from the point of view of the participant. But it underlies his whole conception of faith as he understood it in relation to justification, and it is basic to his conception of faithful and effective participation. It constitutes, therefore, a final and immovable barrier to any unscriptural subjectivizing of the doctrine.

Concluding Estimate

From our brief survey of his teaching, it is immediately apparent that Cranmer was a capable and well-read theologian. He had a vast store of biblical and patristic knowledge upon which he could draw at once in his handling of any point at issue. He had also read and pondered the writings of contemporaries, and he had a mastery of the current forms of theological disputation. Even his administrative preoccupations did not cause him to lose touch with the movements of his age. It is a clear indication of the vitality of his thinking and the honesty of his approach that a man of his age and position should come so late to his final sacramental position.

On the other hand, it must also be apparent that the main strength of Cranmer is in scholarship rather than creative theology. He does not handle many themes at length, but even in the long eucharistic discussion it would be hard to say that he puts forward anything which is genuinely original. His statements are always clear. He brings to them a considerable body of biblical and especially patristic support. He argues them out with acumen. He is obviously responsible in very large measure for the shaping of the new Anglican theology as formularized in the articles and reflected in the Prayer Book. But, through the whole range of his discussions, it is difficult to say that at any single point he made a new contribution to general theological development.

Cranmer is seen at his best, perhaps, in the shorter treatises and especially in the articles. In wider discussion he becomes rather too detailed to be convincing, and like the majority of his contemporaries – and others too – he is far too concerned to score minor points of debate. There are interesting and important passages in the reply to Gardiner, but the *True and Catholic Doctrine* is best read in isolation from the ensuing controversy. Cranmer excelled, of course, in the short but lucid and expressive phrase which gives to the Prayer Book its enduring beauty and freshness. The articles were altered a good deal and in many respects improved in subsequent revisions, but even as they came from Cranmer they are a model of comprehensive but not too vague or generalized formulation. With his alert and not too rigid or dogmatic mind, and his genius for the right formula, Cranmer would have been an invaluable chairman in the ecumenical discussions which he attempted to convene. But circumstances did not allow him to deploy his learning and talents in this sphere as he might have done in a happier age. What he did do was to give to his own church a balanced synopsis of its Reformation convictions. If he was not a theologian of the first rank, he certainly exercised a decisive and lasting influence.

In the teaching itself, certain features stand out which if they are not specifically "Cranmerian" do at least characterize his work. The first of these and in some ways the most outstanding is the patristic emphasis which coloured his whole outlook on current controversies. In some measure, of course, all the reformers appealed to the fathers as well as to Scripture. Zwingli, for example, condemned the traditionalist doctrine of communion, not only because it was not scriptural, but also because he did not find it in the fathers as the first interpreters of Scripture. If necessary, he would have followed Scripture against the fathers, but in most issues he could insist that his teaching was catholic and patristic as well as biblical. On the eucharistic question, Oecolampadius of Basle made a special study of the patristic doctrine. Peter Martyr, too, was a particularly good patristic scholar, as was also Calvin. In England the young Jewel had already set himself to work over the whole range of controverted questions in the light of the patristic literature of the first six centuries. It was a general contention of the reformers that their opponents were the innovators and that they themselves were returning not only to the Bible but to catholic faith and practice. There is, therefore, nothing special or distinctive in the patristic appeal as such. Yet Cranmer does seem to attach a particular value to this appeal and it has a place of especial prominence in almost all his writings. Perhaps it was an innate conservatism. Perhaps it was his mastery of the field. Whatever the reason, the fact itself is indisputable. And it has rather more than a personal importance. For while we cannot speak in any very meaningful way of disciples of Cranmer, there is no doubt that his theological successors in the Church of England have almost all of them manifested this same patristic tendency. They have not all interpreted the fathers in quite the same way as Cranmer did. But they have accepted his appeal to the early church, and for the most part they have used it in opposition to both medieval and modern novelties.

There is another and not unrelated point, that in Cranmer's teaching the incarnation of Christ assumes an importance which we do not always find in Western theology. This emerges particularly in his sacramental doctrine, in which he is obviously feeling after a common incarnational pattern. But it is also important in his understanding of the church and the ministry, and even in a sense of justification, in which there is a duality in the one being of the human actuality on the one hand and the heavenly, or, in Jesus Christ, the divine actuality on the other. He had found this understanding, of course, in some of the fathers, and in his own appreciation of it he may have been influenced to some extent by Peter Martyr, in whom we find the same teaching in much greater detail. Cranmer himself did not work out the theme in any fulness, but it belongs to the very heart of his teaching, and it is an insight which cannot be ignored in any attempt to understand either the life of Christians or their work and witness.

In this respect again Cranmer set the tone for much of the Anglican work which has followed. But he did not make the mistake which has had such unfortunate consequences for some of his successors, especially in recent times. He did not "naturalize" the incarnation by forgetting, ignoring, minimizing, or misinterpreting the redemptive work of Christ in His crucifixion and resurrection. The incarnational principle which he found in sacraments, church, ministry, or justification was not a principle of the natural conjunction of human and divine by virtue of the incarnation. It was a principle only for the redeemed humanity beyond the cross and the tomb. There could be no question, therefore, of a philosophical or natural religion of incarnation, but only of a biblical and redemptive theology. The incarnation as Cranmer saw it has significance, not merely because Christ identified Himself with man, but because He identified Himself with sinful man to bear the judgment of death passed on the old creation and to initiate the new.

The incarnational pattern is, therefore, a pattern only for the word and sacraments of the cross and the resurrection. It is a pattern only for the church which is the company of the redeemed. It is a pattern only for the ministry which is an embassage of reconciliation. It is a pattern only for the Christian life which is a new creation in Jesus Christ. It is a pattern which cannot be given an indiscriminate application, but which can be found only on the far side of Good Friday and Easter Day, in the tension of the old creation and the new. In the resurrection fulfilment, the pattern will be worked out in a new and fuller way, for the church will enjoy in Christ a perfect union of its redeemed humanity and its "divinity": "we shall be like him." But here in the time between regeneration and resurrection, when the union is that of faith, the new life is worked out in terms of sinful flesh, and we know the duality in a sharpness and poignancy of tension. One day, the emphasis will be on the oneness, for the context will be a context of harmony. But for the moment, as Cranmer sees so clearly, the duality is heightened, because it is set in a context of dualism and conflict. The "humanity" of the Christian and the church and the ministry and the word and the sacraments is the sinful humanity with which Christ certainly identified Himself in His incarnation, but which He took to the cross and destroyed in His own body, which for that reason has to be crucified, reckoned dead, put off and finally done to death in physical dissolution. The "divinity" is the new life, life in the Spirit, the life of faith, the new and eternal life which Christ gives us by His rising again from the dead, the life which we have to nourish, into which we have to grow, which we shall know in fulness only in the resurrection, which is itself a union of natures by virtue of the divine-humanity of the resurrected and ascended Christ. It is not in isolation, but in this hard but glorious context of reconciliation that the incarnation has for Cranmer its tremendous significance. To isolate it, and above all to philosophize it, is to be false to the true biblical and evangelical insight which shines steadily in Cranmer's work.

A final point in Cranmer's assessment is his underlying appreciation of the action of the Holy Spirit and therefore of faith. Nowhere does Cranmer give a developed statement of his teaching on the Holy Spirit. But he shows a firm grasp of the fact that the attestation of Christ incarnate, crucified, risen and ascended for us is primarily the work of the Holy Spirit subjectively applying the objective work. Therefore, whether we say church, ministry, word, sacraments or Christian life, we always say Christ, but we say Christ in and by the Holy Spirit. The importance of faith is not as a work, or even as pure subjectivity, but as the operation of the Holy Spirit in which human response is made to the evangelical word and there is the new life of identification with Jesus Christ in death and resurrection. In these matters Cranmer is open to misunderstanding in the light of the current "liberalizing" of Protestant doctrine. But in his own emphasis on the Spirit he has no thought of separating the Spirit from the objective word and work, let alone of "spiritualizing" the action and ultimately the person of the Holy Spirit Himself. Again, he has a proper appreciation of the critical significance of faith, but not in such a way as to give the false prominence to the human subject which involves a final subjectivization. His concern is to give the true and biblical place to that personal application of Christ's work which is specifically the action of the Holy Spirit, operative in word and sacrament to give and nurture the new life which is in Jesus Christ, and therefore to evoke and increase faith.

It has to be recognized, of course, that these positive insights are present in Cranmer only in what we might describe as embryonic form. Cranmer himself was too confined by controversial requirements to develop with any richness an alternative doctrine. We must not judge him too harshly on this account. If the needs of his own time were not always our needs, they were real needs all the same. A living theology always has to reckon with the actualities of the contemporary situation. No reformer could ignore the medieval aberration, or proclaim his message in conscious or unconscious isolation from it. Much of the work had to be negative, and with the current methods of disputation it often had to be tediously and almost pedantically thorough. We certainly cannot afford to be too impatient with this aspect of Cranmer's work. Theology has moved a good deal since those days, but in their codified Tridentine form the doctrines which Cranmer opposed are still a living and potent force on a by no means secondary or unimportant front. It is tiresome to have to traverse continually the same ground, but it is sometimes necessary. If the path is almost tediously well-trodden, it is due to the thoroughness with which Cranmer and his fellow-reformers did the initial work. The hackneyed nature of the material is in itself a tribute.

All the same, the controversial preoccupation did exercise in some ways a hampering or stultifying effect on the development, or at least the expression, of Cranmer's thought. For one thing, it gave to his wider writing an argumentatively negative emphasis. He continually had to meet and overthrow the error and he did not always have enough time or energy adequately to state and discuss the truth. If that is an exaggeration, perhaps we can put it in this way. He could not state and discuss the truth in such a way that it is seen in its right perspective, as a positive thing and not merely the defence against something else. And it cuts rather deeper than that. For even when he does state and discuss the truth, he is inhibited to some extent by the fear of misinterpretation and misunderstanding. The fear was not illusory, for traditionalists like Gardiner did not scruple to turn every possible phrase or expression, to the advantage of their own teaching. But it is not always a help to the free and positive expression of truth to have to keep a continual watch over the shoulder at possible misinterpreters. The whole difficulty in Reformation controversy is precisely at this point. In basis and structure the opposing systems are so similar that the decisive differences may easily be glossed over or overlooked. In these circumstances it is understandable that the reformers should have to be careful in positive construction. But in the long run it is regrettable and even harmful. For after all, the best answer to error, even to the error which is a perversion of the truth, is not a negative critique of the error, but a bold affirmation of the truth. It is not enough merely to show the falsity of transubstantiation. It must also and primarily be shown what is the real and essential truth of which this doctrine is an elaborately but basically misconceived expression. In the long run, it is this part of the task which is the more important, as Cranmer realized with his bold title: *The True and Catholic Doctrine.* But in the ensuing discussion, it did not have always the more dominant, which is the obvious and rightful, emphasis.

Yet when that is said, and every reasonable criticism is accepted, the theology of Cranmer cannot be dismissed as merely negative or even derivative. He was not a great creative theologian. He did allow himself to be too much hampered by the petty dialectics of scholastic controversy. But he did something more than give a learned apologia for the rejection of traditionalist teaching, and a concise summary of the new position. He also showed in his works a clear and bold understanding of the great themes which were his primary concern. Indeed, if he himself did not always work them out, we find in Cranmer the basic insights which will control a genuinely biblical and evangelical reconstruction.

Select Bibliography

Books of primary importance for wider reading.

H. Bullinger, *Decades*, Ed. Parker Society, 1849-52
J. Calvin, *Institutes*, Eng. tr. Beveridge, 1845
T. Cranmer, *Works*, Ed. Jenkins, 4 vols., 1833
___, ibid, Ed. Parker Society, 2 vols., 1844-6[1]
Formularies of Faith under Henry VIII, Ed. Lloyd, Oxford, 1856
J. Foxe, *Acts and Monuments*, Ed. Townsend, 8 vols.
M. Luther, *Werke*, Weimar edition
___, *Narratives of the Reformation*
___, *Original Letters*, Ed. Parker Society, 2 vols., 1846-7*
N. Ridley, *Works*, Ed. Parker Society, 1841*
H. Zwingli, *Werke*, Corpus Reformatorum
___, *Selected Writings*, Library of Christian Classics, vol. 24, 1953

Secondary Books

G.W. Bromiley, *Thomas Cranmer*, London, 1955
A.C. Deane, *The Life of Thomas Cranmer*, London, 1927
G. Dix, *The Shape of the Liturgy*, 1944
F.E. Hutchinson, *Thomas Cranmer and the English Reformation*, London, 1951
A.D. Innes, *Cranmer and the Reformation in England*, 1900
A.J. Mason, *Thomas Cranmer*, London, 1898
A.F. Pollard, *Thomas Cranmer* (Heroes of the Reformation Series)
C.C. Richardson, *Zwingli and Cranmer on the Eucharist* (*Cranmer dixit et contradixit*), Evanston, 1949
F.J. Smithen, *Continental Protestantism and the English Reformation*, London, 1927
C.H. Smyth, *Cranmer and the Reformation under Edward VI*, Cambridge, 1926
J. Strype, *Annals of the Reformation*, 4 vols.
___, *Ecclesiastical Memorials*, 3 vols.
___, *Memorials of Thomas Cranmer*, 3 vols.
G.B. Timms, *Dixit Cranmer*, Alcuin Club Papers, 1946

---

1. In the text the abbreviation P.S. is used to indicate the Parker Society editions.

Index of Subjects

Baptism,
  ceremonies in, 57-8
  of infants, 57, 63
  presence of Christ in, 59
  work of, 60-1

Church,
  authority of, 18, 20 f.
  inerrancy of, 44-5
  marks of true, 46 f.
  sectarianism, 43
  true and false, 42 f.

Eucharistic presence,
  distinction of natures, 73
  faithful reception, 77
  Holy Spirit and, 76, 79, 82
  incarnation and atonement, 79 f.
  real presence, 71
  sacramental presence, 74-5
  spiritual presence, 76
  transubstantiation, 70

Eucharistic work,
  faith, 94 f.
  Holy Spirit, 88, 91 f.
  nourishment, 89 f.
  sacrifice, 84 f.
  sacrificial response, 87-8

Justification,
  antinomianism, 34
  atonement, 31
  faith, 32
  faith only, 32
  nature of faith, 33
  works of faith, 34

Ministry,
  appointment of ministers, 50-1
  bishops and priests, 51
  marriage of clergy, 49
  sacrament of orders, 49-50
  threefold ministry, 49

Scripture,
  apostles, 20
  canon, 18
  ceremonies, 17, 20 f.
  church, 13 f., 18, 20 f.
  fathers, 16 f., 22 f., 98-9
  Papacy, 14
  supremacy of, 13
  tradition, 16 f., 25 f.

Index of Names

Ab Ulmis, 6
Ambrose, 29, 35
Ann Boleyn, xii
Anne of Cleves, xii, xv
Anselm, 16, 29
Aquinas, 16, 29
Athanasius, 16, 18
Augustine, 16, 24, 29, 35, 57, 63, 72, 77, 95

Basil, 16, 29
Berengarius, 90
Bernard, 29
Bradford, 3
Brooks, 69
Bucer, xxi, xxiv, xxv, 5
Bullinger, xxi

Calvin, xxi, 7, 10, 36, 54, 98
Campeggio, ix
Cecil, viii, xxvii
Cheke, xxvii
Chrysostom, 29, 35
Colet, viii
Coverdale, xiv
Cranmer,
  articles, forty-two, xxvii
    six, xv
    ten, xiii
  birth and education, vii
  Bishops' Book, xiii
  church spoliation, xiii, xxiv, 10
  continental contacts, xx-xxi
  "divorce," etc., ix f.
  doctrine,
    baptism, 57 f.
    church, 18 f, 42 f.
    eucharistic presence, 69 f.
    eucharistic work, 84 f.
    justification, 28 f.
    ministry, 48 f.
    Scripture, 12 f.
  English Bible, xiv-xv
  King's Book, xxvii
  Litany, xvii
  marriages, vii, x
  martyrdom, xviii
  ordinal, xxiii
  Prayer Books, xxi, xxv
  scholarship, 1 f.
  writings, 6 f.
Cromwell, xiii, xiv, xv, xvi
Cyprian, 16, 18, 24

Damplip, 69

Edward VI, xxvii, 7
Emissenus, 61, 87
Erasmus, viii, xix, 5, 12

Fagius, xxi, 5
Fisher, 12
Fox, ix
Foxe, 3, 69

Gardiner, ix, xi, xviii, xxii, 4, 5, 30, 58, 59, 91-2, 94, 97, 102
Gostwicke, xvi
Grindal, 3

Henry VIII, ix f., xi f., xvi, xviii, 4, 5, 14, 49, 69
Hilary, 80
Hooker, xxiv
Hooper, xviii, xxiii, 6

Irenaeus, 16, 29

Jerome, 16, 28
Jewel, 3, 23, 69, 98

Index of Names

John A Lasco, xxi
Justus Jonas, xx, 1, 69

Katherine of Aragon, ix f., 14
Katherine HOWARD, xii, xv
Knox, xxiv, xxvi

Lambert, 69
Latimer, xxiv
Lombard, 29
Luther, viii, 7, 12, 18, 28, 33, 36, 53, 65

Mary, xxvii, 23, 54
Melanchthon, xxi, 14
Morice, 3

Northumberland, xxii, xxiii, xxvi
Nowell, 30

Ochino, xxi
Oecolampadius, 70, 98
Origen, 16, 29
Osiander, x

Parker, 3
Peter MARTYR, xx, 5, 6

Pole, x
Ponet, 7

Ridley, xx, xxiv, xxv, 3 n., 2, 4, 5-6, 70, 98, 99

Scotus, 16
Smith, xxii, 42, 45
Somerset, xix, xxii

Tertullian, 16, 58
Theodoret, 29
Tremellius, xxi
Tunstall, xxiv
Tyndale, xiv

Vadian, 69
Vigilius, 73

Warham, xi, xii, xiii
Whitgift, xxiv
Wolsey, vii, 2
Woolton, 30

Zwingli, 7, 10, 12, 36, 70, 90, 98

You may also be interested in:

Baptism and the Anglican Reformers

by G.W. Bromiley

Writing in the middle of the twentieth century, G.W. Bromiley was acutely aware of the renewal of debates surrounding baptism taking place within the Anglican church and elsewhere. These debates, which are still the cause of denominational division, can be best understood by tracing them back to their origins in the sixteenth century. Analysing the Anglican Reformers' views on baptism's sacramental status, its liturgical format and its theological substance, Bromiley places the current diversity of positions in its proper context. The legitimacy of infant baptism, the authority of ministers and the efficacy of grace are all discussed. Whether a scholar of ecclesiological and doctrinal history, or of the current debate within and between churches, this study is essential reading on the question of baptism past and present.

A comprehensive exposition of English Reformation views on Baptism and their relevance today

Geoffrey W. Bromiley (1915-2009) was Professor of Church History and Historical Theology at Fuller Theological Seminary. He gained his MA at Cambridge and his PhD and Dlitt in Edinburgh, and was previously lecturer and vice principal at Tyndale Hall, Bristol, and Rector of St Thomas' Episcopal Church, Edinburgh. Among his substantial output are his *Introduction to the Theology of Karl Barth*; *Historical Theology: An Introduction*; and *Thomas Cranmer, Theologian* (James Clarke & Co.).

Published 2023

Hardback ISBN: 978 0 227 17868 3
Paperback ISBN: 978 0 227 17867 6
PDF ISBN: 978 0 227 17870 6
ePub ISBN: 978 0 227 17869 0

You may also be interested in:

The Institution of a Christian Man

Edited by Gerald Bray

Compiled during the early years of the Reformation, The Institution of a Christian Man lays out the principles of the nascent Church of England. In his definitive new edition, Gerald Bray charts the development of this text from the first version introduced by Archbishop Thomas Cranmer and his cohort of bishops, to the extensive edits made by Henry VIII himself, and finally to the version written by Bishop Edmund Bonner under the radically different circumstances of Mary I's reign.

By combining the Bishops' Book and the King's Book into a single text – rather than in sequence – Bray shows which sections were added, deleted, and retained throughout the revisions. This process allows the reader to reconstruct the texts and, at the same time, follow the process by which one was transformed into the other. Bishop Bonner's Book, which appears separately, illustrates additional changes and elaborations from the previous two books. Such a comparative study in a user-friendly and accessible style has never been published before.

> *'The three official statements of faith produced under Henry VIII and Mary Tudor are at last given the full scholarly treatment they have long cried out for. . . . Every historian of the English Reformation will want to keep this wonderfully easy-to-use edition within arm's reach.* – **Alec Ryrie**, Durham University

Reverend Dr Gerald Bray has a PhD from Paris-Sorbonne. He worked as Professor of Anglican Studies at Beeson Divinity School, and is now a Research Professor for the same institution. He is also Director of Research at the Latimer Trust. His other publications with James Clarke & Co Ltd include *Documents of the English Reformation* (1994; 2nd edition 2004) and *The Books of Homilies: A Critical Edition* (2016).

Published 2018

Hardback ISBN: 978 0 227 17668 9
Paperback ISBN: 978 0 227 17670 2
PDF ISBN: 978 0 227 90642 2
ePub ISBN: 978 0 227 90643 9